Forced Out

FORCED OUT

*The Fate of Polish Jewry
in Communist Poland*

Arthur J. Wolak

Forced Out: The Fate of Polish Jewry in Communist Poland

Grateful acknowledgment for permission to reprint maps (pp. 14 and 25) from Tatiana Klonowicz and Grażyna Wieczorkowska, eds. *Social Change: Adaptation and Resistance* (Warsaw, Poland: Warsaw University, Institute for Social Studies Press, 2002). The author also wishes to thank Martin Gilbert for permission to reprint a map (p. 13) from *The Routledge Atlas of Jewish History*, 6th ed. (London and New York: Routledge, 2003).

9030

Cover photo taken by the author in Warsaw, Poland's historic Stare Miasto (Old Town). The city square, destroyed during World War II, was painstakingly rebuilt according to prewar plans. All interior photos except those on pp. 44 and 121 were taken by the author.

Published by Fenestra Books®
610 East Delano Street, Suite 104
Tucson, Arizona 85705 U.S.A.
www.fenestrabooks.com

Publisher's Cataloging-in-Publication Data
(Provided by Quality Books, Inc.)

Wolak, Arthur J.
    Forced out : the fate of Polish Jewry in communist
Poland / Arthur J. Wolak.
    p. cm.
    Includes bibliographical references and index.
    LCCN 2003116457
    ISBN 1587362910

    1. Jews—Persecutions—Poland. 2. Antisemitism—
Poland—History—20th century. 3. Poland—Politics and
government—1945–1980. I. Title.

DS135.P6W56 2004   323.1'19'240438
                    QBI03-200963

*To my mother
and
in memory of my father,
who triumphed over adversity in Poland
before, during, and after the war*

Contents

Preface ix
Introduction 1

1. Poland and the Jews 15
2. Anti-Semitism in Poland 33
3. The 1967 Middle East Crisis 45
4. Poland's Assault on the Jews, 1967–68 57
5. Political Opportunism and Anti-Semitism 75
6. The "Zionist" Scapegoats 89
7. Exile of Jews 109
8. Political Anti-Semitism in Communist Poland 127
9. From Persecution to Acceptance 141

Afterword 163
Notes 167
Bibliography 183
Index 195

MAPS

The Jews of Central Europe, 1000–1500 13
*Poland's Territorial Changes, from the
Tenth to Twentieth Century* 14
Poland after the Eighteenth-Century Partitions 25

Preface

Among the Polish political leadership's most profound failures during the tumultuous period of Communist rule was not its inability to protect all citizens from organized state oppression, but its actual targeting of a particular group—citizens of Jewish ancestry—for state-directed tyranny. Carried out at the very top of the Communist hierarchy and vigorously pursued throughout Polish society, the plan relied on an age-old method to direct popular discontent away from the true source of domestic problems—the nation's leadership itself—while attempting to secure the support of the masses and ensure the regime's political survival. Not only did this tactic epitomize the abuse of state power, but it also defied Poland's own constitutional guarantees prohibiting such mistreatment.

This book identifies and examines the influences that led to the 1967–68 "anti-Zionist" campaign that targeted Poland's small population of citizens of Jewish ancestry for state-sanctioned harassment. Since the Polish government's overt persecution of Jews fulfilled domestic political aims, the guiding objective in the pages that follow is to place the actions of 1967–68 in context of the postwar Jewish experience in Poland and the Soviet Union with reference to the geopolitical, social, and temporal influences that directly and indirectly contributed to the events described herein.

Besides exploring relevant domestic economic and political problems that contributed to the Polish regime's use of anti-Semitism as a political weapon, attention is given to Soviet anti-Jewish policies and tactics for their influence on the relentless storm of political anti-Semitism that swept across Poland in the late 1960s. This political anti-Semitism did not conclude until the majority of Jews who had chosen to remain in Poland and help rebuild the nation following the Second World War had been, in no uncertain terms, effectively evicted from the country.

Given Poland's long history as a principled nation with numerous examples of respect for the protection of minority rights, the specific policy pursued by Poland's Communist leadership in the late 1960s was appalling. Long before the events of 1967–68, Poland had experienced centuries of challenges, both to its geographical frontiers and to its political status in Europe. During the late Middle Ages, the Polish kingdom resembled others in Europe. But as Poland grew in size and power it transformed into a Polish-Lithuanian Commonwealth and became a prosperous realm. By the sixteenth century, Poland had proven its difference from other countries of Europe through the absence of religious wars and support of religious tolerance. Indeed, the principle of toleration of 1573 enacted by Poland's monarchs was among the most significant advances in Europe. In the seventeenth century, however, despite successful defenses against Sweden, Russia, and Turkey, and participation in wars in the Ukraine against Bogdan Chmielnicki's Cossacks—after which Russia built up its empire and Prussia expanded—Poland fell under Russian control. This was not the last time in Poland's history that a Russian conquest would occur, as the twentieth century later proved.

Poland's disappearance from the map of Europe in 1795—the result of Western cooperation with Eastern strategists to transform Europe based on their belief that European anarchy could be blamed on the continued existence of a Polish nation—inspired revolutionaries in the nineteenth century and beyond. Following the First World War, Poland once more emerged as an independent nation—*Rzeczpospolita Polska*, or Republic of Poland— helped by the population's widespread identification with Polish culture, language, and history. At that momentous time, Poles were eager to fight to reconstruct their country, just as they would be after the Second World War. However, in 1944 external forces again decided the fate of Poland, which remained a Soviet satellite state—*Polska Rzeczpospolita Ludowa*, or People's Republic of Poland— for most of the next half century.

Poland may have regained statehood but it did not regain sovereignty as it was subjected to Communist transformation directed by the Kremlin. Nonetheless, Poland's desire for independence saw popular uprisings among both workers and the intelligentsia between 1956 and 1989, ultimately leading to the effective dismantling of the oppressive Soviet-inspired Communist regime. Indeed, toward the dawn of the twenty-first century Poland emerged as the effective leader of change among nations of the former Eastern Bloc. After the fall of Communist rule in 1989, a new era in Polish domestic life was launched that Polish citizens still must confront, accommodate, and accept in order to succeed in a Europe once again undergoing rapid change.

In the 1990s Poland cultivated new political allegiances and firmly attached itself to the West. The nation embraced democratic principles, joined the NATO military alliance for border stability, and sought membership in the European Union for a stable economic future. Now that the EU has embraced Poland as part of its strategic third-millennium eastward expansion, Poles must come to terms with their nation's past, both its achievements and recent failures, not least of which being the reprehensible events of 1967–68. Poles will also need to embark upon an essential process of introspection to understand their nation's identity so that it can be preserved within the new powerful bloc of European nations. To successfully move forward, therefore, Poland must conquer the daunting challenge of reconciling its history of openness and toleration with its Communist-era isolationism and repression, particularly with regard to the treatment of its Jewish population. Hence, the position of the small community of Jews who remain in post-Communist Poland is briefly considered, since how the Jews are viewed by the general population and are treated by the state will prove crucial for Poland's successful reconciliation with its past as it strives toward a better and more stable future.

In *Forced Out* my intent is to provide readers with a summary not only of what took place in Poland in the postwar era, which resulted in the almost complete close to centuries of continuous Jewish presence on Polish soil, but also of the political and career implications for those who pursued this policy to its unjust conclusion. If readers learn something new about a period that has not received much coverage in history classrooms, or acquire some insights into the evils of political anti-Semitism and the dangers of totalitarianism, then this book has more than served its purpose.

୶

Raised in the peaceful democracy of Canada rather than the totalitarian Communist Poland from which my parents fled, my curiosity about Poland's tumultuous period of 1967–68 began with stories I heard from people who had left Poland during the postwar era, an interest that grew as a result of personal visits to Poland and research I undertook while pursuing graduate studies in history.

My late father, Dr. Edward Wolak, a physician and senior epidemiologist in Poland's postwar health administration, understood very well the precarious position of the Jews in Poland. His early recognition of the potential dangers of Poland's regime and consequent emigration during Poland's Stalinist era ultimately convinced my mother, among Poland's leading choral conductors, to begin life anew in the West. I want to express my appreciation to my parents for their great efforts to ensure that their sons were raised far away from the totalitarian state whence they emigrated, which, if only indirectly, led to the writing of this book. I owe a special debt of gratitude to my mother, Elizabeth Wolak, for her close readings of the manuscript and assistance with translations of Polish sources.

For sparking my particular interest in Poland's difficult era of 1967–68, I must express my appreciation to Professor Józef Parnas (1909–1998)—a colleague and lifelong friend of my father—who was among Poland's most high-profile victims of the anti-Semitic campaign. While in Copenhagen, Denmark I was fortunate to discuss many topics with Dr. Parnas, including Poland's postwar Communist regime and his experience as one of its targets. His vivid description gave my later research and writing greater clarity.

—*Arthur J. Wolak*

Introduction

The fate of east European Jewry had been determined by the Holocaust; it could never again be the center of world Jewry. The establishment of Israel provided a new focus. After 1945 many of the survivors of the Holocaust were drawn there and in Eastern Europe Communist parties anxious to make use of traditional popular anti-Semitism (not least in the Soviet Union) had encouraged emigration by harrying and minor persecution. In some countries the outcome was a virtual elimination of the Jewish population as a significant element in the demography of the region. Poland was the outstanding example.

– John M. Roberts, *A History of Europe*

Reflecting on the momentous events that occurred in Eastern Europe in 1968, the world's memory tends to focus on the aftermath of Czechoslovakia's "Prague Spring," when Alexander Dubček's policy of economic and political liberalization was crushed in the month of August by a Soviet-led invasion that restored oppressive Communist totalitarianism in the Soviet sphere of influence. Just as ominous, however, were the events that took place in Poland between 1967 and 1968. Although no invasion was launched from outside Poland to quell rising anti-Communist sentiments, the Polish government carried out fierce repressive measures to achieve this aim from within.

Among the actions seemingly intended to strengthen Communist control inside the People's Republic of Poland was the nefarious policy to eliminate members of a spe-

1

cific ethnic group—Poles of Jewish descent—from positions of influence within Polish society. Emanating from
the leadership of the ruling Communist Party of Poland,
the anti-Zionist rhetoric that swept across the country
during 1967–68—also a feature of the 1968 pro-Soviet
clampdown on Czechoslovakia's reform-minded regime[1]—led to severe reprisals against Jewish citizens of
Poland, culminating in their effective expulsion. The
majority of Jews who had remained in Poland following
the Second World War emigrated as a consequence of the
Polish government's anti-Semitic campaign.

While the reprehensible actions that took place in
Poland during 1967–68 were fundamentally unjust, they
were not new, original, or unprecedented. Whether the
Near East of biblical times, or Europe and Russia of the
twentieth century, throughout history Jews have been victims of rampant persecution, including state-imposed dis-
criminatory policies, widespread massacres, and expulsions from numerous jurisdictions. Until the modern era,
however, Poland had been among the few politically tolerant European nations in which the Jews had lived. That
the authorities of a country that once welcomed and protected the Jews would, centuries later, force them out is
indeed one of the sad ironies of European history.

This chronicle of Poland—the period from 1967
through 1968—has not received much attention in general surveys of European history, either because this particular era is still too recent to have made the pages of popular history books, or because for many popular twentieth-century European history writers, attention to the
Jewish experience in Poland tends to begin and end with
the Holocaust. The latter reason is understandable since
global awareness of the Nazi genocide of the Jews is
essential, not only so the sins of the past are not repeated
but so they are never forgotten for the profound lessons

they contain about immorality, intolerance, injustice, and inhumanity.

As a reflection of relatively recent history, however, this account has much to offer. What may not be widely known to general readers is that the Jewish presence in Poland did not end with the evils perpetrated by the Nazis largely on Polish soil during the Second World War. While most Holocaust survivors chose to emigrate, a small but significant number of Poles of Jewish ancestry chose to stay in Poland following the Second World War. One such Polish Jew was Władysław Szpilman, the Polish pianist whose autobiographical account of his survival in Warsaw during the Nazi occupation, *The Pianist*, was transformed into a widely acclaimed, internationally award-winning motion picture by Roman Polański, himself a Holocaust survivor who, like most Jews of his generation, left Poland in the decades following the war.[2]

One evening during a visit to Poland in the autumn of 2002, I sat in a Warsaw movie theater and watched *The Pianist*. It was a packed house comprised of curious Poles who saw a chapter of their nation's past depicted onscreen. Larger numbers of Poles—among others throughout Europe and the rest of the world—should also see this film, for it will remind them of a people who populated Poland in significant numbers before the Nazi genocide, followed just two decades later by Poland's Communist regime's fierce domestic campaign of coerced emigration, virtually wiped them out.

The significance of Szpilman's story is multifaceted. While it depicts one man's survival during the Holocaust, it also reveals a postwar Jewish presence in Poland that cannot be denied. A portrayal of the horrors of the Holocaust, this film also depicts a Jewish individual who remained in Poland after the war for his own reasons, to continue his musical career, adding much to Poland's postwar culture through his innumerable compositions and stage and radio performances.

Although the Jewish population that stayed on in postwar Poland did not reflect or replicate the thriving Jewish religious scholarship and social culture prevalent in Poland for centuries prior to the outbreak of the Second World War, this was neither within their ability, due to the overwhelming destruction of Jewish life, nor was it their intent. Their reasons for remaining in Poland after the war reflected many different motives, from shared ideological and political beliefs on the one hand, to non-political but cultural, linguistic, occupational, or emotional attachment to the country of their birth on the other.

Despite the small number of Jews residing in postwar Poland relative to the number that resided in Poland before the war, their impact on Poland, as Szpilman exemplifies, was never trivial. This book is therefore about what ultimately happened to the majority of Jews who remained in Communist Poland in the decades following the Second World War. This era of Polish and general history should not be forgotten, for it holds valuable lessons about the evils of state persecution and the inherent dangers of totalitarian regimes. As such, Poland's 1967–68 "anti-Zionist" campaign deserves a hard-earned position in the files of twentieth-century injustices.

While it is not the intent of this book to suggest that Jews were the sole victims of the Polish government's repressive policies of 1967–68—since non-Jewish opponents of the Polish regime also suffered from the government's oppressive actions—this book focuses on the Polish leadership's specific exploitation of political anti-Semitism in its efforts to manipulate the masses toward its favor. As a consequence, why and how Poles of Jewish origin were specifically targeted for persecution by the Polish government during the final years of the Gomułka administration are fundamental questions these pages attempt to answer.

৵

Launched under the pretext of "anti-Zionism" following Israel's victory over Arab nations during June 1967's Six-Day War and intensified after the March 1968 outbreak of student demonstrations against the existing Communist government, the anti-Jewish campaign that consumed Poland is a shameful period in Poland's recent history. This period in which Jews and intellectuals became victims of the Polish government's relentless campaign of harassment, incarceration, and forced emigration has become synonymous with the label "March." Such an innocent name of a month underscores the Polish tradition of referring to "dramatic historical punctuation marks" by the months in which they occurred.[3] Looking back at "March 1968," this label undeniably evokes the era of crisis to which it refers.

Since this book's purpose is to account for the underlying reasons for the appalling political witch-hunt that began in June 1967 and accelerated in March 1968, the context of Poland's anti-Semitic campaign is explored to discern how Polish anti-Semitism, opposing factions within the Communist Polish United Workers' Party (PUWP), the outcome of the Six-Day War, and Soviet policy toward the Middle East, Soviet Jews, and Poland contributed to a social climate that led the Polish government to conclude that unleashing its nefarious policy against the Jews of Poland was politically advantageous.

Although Poland's rulers articulated a policy of "anti-Zionism" in 1967–68, it could not be interpreted in any other way than thinly veiled anti-Semitism for reasons of political opportunism. After all, anti-Zionism connotes anti-Semitism, because if anti-Zionist policies were ever to succeed, Israel's overwhelmingly Jewish population would not survive, a fearful outcome that is the ultimate aim of the most extreme adherents of anti-Semitism.[4]

Austrian journalist Wilhelm Marr first used the term "anti-Semitism" in 1879 to denigrate Jews. But the particular hatred for the Jews to whom the word anti-Semitism would subsequently refer went back a millennium and a half to Roman Emperor Constantine's embrace of the new faith of Christianity and the Christians' subsequent control of the apparatus of the state.[5] The clear inference whenever the word "anti-Semitism" is used, therefore, is that the target is the Jew, for despite some who maintain that "Semite" represents both Arab and Jew, all anti-Semites have directed their wrath exclusively against Jews. Hence, whether "anti-Semitism," "anti-Zionism," or other words are used as euphemisms for the hatred of Jews, they are all equally dangerous because of their shared implications. The use of euphemisms inside Communist Poland, which exhibited many of the defining criteria of a totalitarian state, made the situation even more dangerous.

In totalitarian environments such as Communist Poland, not only is the individual subordinated to the state, but opposition to political and cultural expression is also suppressed wherein the political authority exercises absolute and centralized control over all aspects of life. Since minority groups face a greater probability of being mistreated by a regime possessing unrivaled power over domestic media and possessing sufficient manpower and bureaucratic efficiency to carry out any policy, no matter how evil, a second aim of this book is to remind readers of the dangerous consequences of totalitarianism, whereby a regime of seeming invincibility systematically chokes all opposition to control every aspect of a nation's life, its military, economy, religion, schools, and press. In the late

1960s, the treatment by Poland's Communist leadership of dissenting intellectuals and, in particular, Poland's citizens of Jewish ancestry, epitomized these dangerous consequences.

At the close of an eventful century and an even more eventful millennium, it would be reasonable to expect that sophisticated nations would have reached a consensus that persecution on ethnic and religious grounds should neither be committed by any government nor tolerated by any society. Yet innumerable examples throughout the world confirm that many nations still commit grievous offenses against humanity—for selfish political objectives or out of malice—with or without the support of the masses. Notorious twentieth-century campaigns to annihilate Jews and Armenians occurred before the 1960s; however, attacks against Cambodians, Iraqi Kurds, Bosnians, and Rwandans are familiar examples of tragedies that took place since the 1970s. They should have been prevented or stopped as soon as they began, if not by the regimes carrying out the harassment or the citizens within, then by the outside world. Therefore, the persecution of Poland's Jews in the late 1960s, which occurred despite the Jews' well-known history of suffering, highlights the precarious position of minorities in any totalitarian society that lacks the appropriate safeguards to ensure human rights are respected.

Why Did Poland's 1967–68 Anti-Semitic Campaign Happen?

During the Communist rule of Poland, the change from concealed unofficial prejudice to institutionalized political anti-Semitism can only be understood as the result of particular historical, national, and political experiences that occurred within a specific Polish context. The following pages, therefore, provide direct and indirect explanations of the domestic and international circumstances that contributed to the launch of Poland's shameful policy.

A key argument this book makes is that Israel's victory in the Six-Day War served as a convenient excuse for Poland's political leadership to initiate an "anti-Zionist" policy in conformance with the Soviet Union's policy of Arab favoritism. But this is only part of the story. Why would this course of action have proven beneficial to the Polish regime? First, given traditional Polish anti-Semitism, Poland's political leadership likely believed that Poles would be receptive to propaganda identifying Poland's Jews as a domestic threat based on their presumed loyalty to Israel; second, articulating a vigorous "anti-Zionist" stance would conform to Soviet dictates and therefore enhance Poland's image as a reliable member of the Soviet Bloc; lastly, this extreme policy could thwart disunity among large segments within the Polish Communist Party, particularly by appeasing an influential special interest group of the Polish United Workers' Party, which addressed a specific domestic concern of the regime. Hence, the exploitation of traditional Polish anti-Semitism ultimately served to fortify popular support for Poland's Communist regime, or so the Polish political leadership of the era had hoped.

In order to understand these influences, this book starts from the beginning and acquaints readers with an overview of the Jewish people's political status in Poland from the time Jews first began arriving in significant numbers until the 1967–68 anti-Semitic campaign (**chapters 1 and 2**). The context of the 1967 Middle East crisis and Poland's response is examined while exploring the impact of Soviet policies on the Middle East, Zionism, and Soviet Jewry to assess how they created a climate that helped make Poland's 1967–68 anti-Jewish campaign possible (**chapter 3**). The campaign of political anti-Semitism that was unleashed in Poland following the 1967 Six-Day War is then considered in detail.

Though Poland's domestic economic and political problems were catalysts for the public's growing displeasure with the existing Communist regime—and the regime's corresponding tendency to blame Jews for these troubles—primary focus is centered on the leadership of Poland's Communist Party, the PUWP, and the pressure of internal rivalries within the Party on policy decisions to determine their collective impact on Gomułka's actions and the formation and implementation of Poland's anti-Jewish policy in 1967–68 (**chapter 4**). Gomułka's role is explored further, along with the attempt of Moczar and his followers to undermine Gomułka's leadership position, to show how the campaign's organized provocation to incite Poles against Jews was intended to divert the attention of the masses from their daily problems and increase their support for the existing political leadership (**chapter 5**).

Examining the Soviet Union's influence on Poland's domestic policies helps put Poland's use of political anti-Semitism in context. Stalin's efforts to exploit the Jews to facilitate his control of Eastern Europe provided a powerful and ominous foundation for subsequent political anti-Semitism (**chapter 6**). In order to understand the significance of specific tactics employed by the Polish regime, therefore, Soviet examples are considered to illustrate what lessons Communist Poland learned from its powerful and oppressive neighbor to the east. These Polish repressive tactics, and their Soviet models, are further clarified by a study of the treatment of Professor Józef Parnas, a high-profile victim of Poland's anti-Semitic purge (**chapter 7**).

Following the detailed description of what occurred in Poland in 1967–68 and the various influences that contributed to the launch of a policy of political anti-Semitism (**chapters 1–7**), salient aspects of the Polish government's 1967–68 anti-Semitic campaign are summarized to help put this indefensible period of Poland's recent history into broader perspective. The fate of the main perpetrators and victims of the Polish regime's infamous anti-Semitic campaign is also described (**chapter 8**).

In the aftermath of Poland's oppressive policies of the 1960s, the situation of Polish Jewry following the 1967–68 era and its attempts to rebuild from a position of virtual ruin is touched upon. We speculate on the future of Polish Jewry within a post-Communist nation that is working at a feverish pace to emulate the ideals, policies, and successes of the Western democracies with whom Poland is becoming increasingly allied politically, militarily, economically, and culturally (**chapter 9**). Poland's current transformation is a strong reflection of the evolutionary and revolutionary process that first began during Poland's earliest years under the Polish kings and has continued in one form or another until today. Indeed, the Jews of Poland have witnessed these changes and experienced the consequences to their way of life over the course of nine tumultuous centuries.

Looking closely at this momentous era in modern Polish history, Poland's 1967–68 anti-Semitic campaign depended on the volatile combination of four pivotal conditions that made the singling out of Poles of Jewish origin a clear example of manipulative political opportunism. These four dynamic, powerful, and distinctive circumstances include:

- The outcome of the 1967 Six-Day War

- A bitter rivalry between opposing factions within Poland's ruling Communist Party

- The tacit approval of the leadership of the Soviet Union

- Longstanding popular anti-Semitic sentiments in Poland

Considering that Poland's Communist regime's fierce campaign against Poland's Jews had multiple influences, it may prove helpful for readers to consider the chapters in this book as a series of responses to several fundamental questions about the Polish regime's 1967–68 anti-Semitic campaign that reflect two central perspectives—domestic and international influences.

The Polish domestic context—Although less overt anti-Jewish measures were taken during the Communist era since the late 1940s, the extreme measures taken by the Polish regime in the late 1960s require answers to the following questions to understand what occurred and why:

- Was the Polish government's sudden, dramatic, and overt political oppression of the Jews a natural outgrowth of preexisting anti-Semitic sentiments within the Communist Party and Polish society, or a new phenomenon? **(chapters 1–3)**

- Did the policy of singling out a defenseless minority following the 1967 Middle East war serve strategic interests of the Polish government? **(chapters 2–5 and 7)**

- Was Władysław Gomułka largely to blame for initiating or sanctioning the policy, or was it taken to its extreme conclusion by Mieczysław Moczar, together with other ostensibly anti-Semitic Party members, who seized the opportunity presented by Gomułka's public anti-Zionist statements in the immediate aftermath of the Six-Day War? (**chapters 4, 5,** and **8**)

International or external influences—Since the Soviet-sponsored Arab nations were decisively defeated by Israel during the Six-Day War, and the authority of Poland's Communist government largely depended on the Soviet Union's support, answers to the following questions are critically important to assess the power of external pressures on the implementation of Poland's national strategy:

- Was Poland's domestic policy toward the Jews merely an extension of the Soviet Union's own domestic and Middle Eastern policy? (**chapter 3**)

- Did the Polish government initiate the anti-Semitic campaign independent of Soviet influence? (**chapters 6** and **7**)

This book attempts to answer these challenging questions in order to assess the domestic and international circumstances that guided the Polish leadership's plan and launch of the 1967–68 anti-Semitic campaign, and to understand the subtle causes for what transpired in Poland during the late 1960s, among the most turbulent eras in the history of Polish Communist rule.

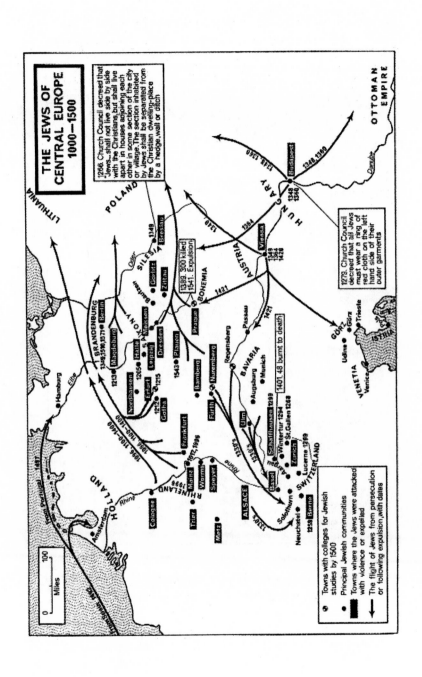

THE JEWS OF
CENTRAL EUROPE
1000—1500

1266 Church Council decreed that "Jews...shall not live side by side with the Christians, but shall live apart in houses adjoining each other in some section of the city or village. The section inhabited by Jews shall be separated from the Christian dwelling-place by a hedge, wall or ditch

1279. Church Council decreed that all Jews must wear a ring of red cloth on the left hand side of their outer garments

1389. 300 killed. 1541. Expulsion

1401. 48 burnt to death

LITHUANIA
POLAND
SILESIA
BRANDENBURG
SAXONY
BOHEMIA
AUSTRIA
BAVARIA
HUNGARY
RHINELAND
ALSACE
SWITZERLAND
HOLLAND
VENETIA
ISTRIA
OTTOMAN EMPIRE

Hamburg
Berlin
Magdeburg
Breslau
Görlitz
Zittau
Bautzen
Halle
Leipzig
Dresden
Prague
Pilsen
Vienna
Budapest
Görz
Udine
Görz
Trieste
Venice
Passau
Regensburg
Munich
Augsburg
Nuremberg
Bamberg
Fürth
Ulm
Schaffhausen
Winterthur
St. Gallen
Zurich
Lucerne
Basel
Solothurn
Berne
Neuchâtel
Frankfurt
Cologne
Trier
Mainz
Worms
Speyer
Mainz
Northeim
Erfurt
Gotha

Danube
Elbe
Oder
Rhine
Rhône

Principal Jewish communities
Towns where the Jews were attacked with violence or expelled
The flight of Jews from persecution or following expulsion, with dates
Towns with colleges for Jewish studies by 1500

0   100
Miles

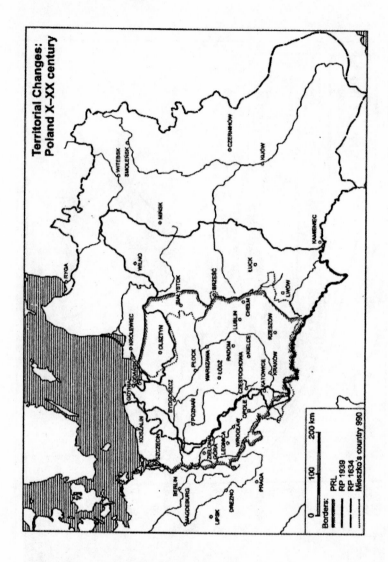

Territorial Changes: Poland X–XX century

Borders:
PRL
RP 1939
RP 1634
Mieszko's country 990

RP: *Rzeczpospolita Polska* (Republic of Poland)
PRL: *Polska Rzeczpospolita Ludowa* (People's Republic of Poland)

The current borders of Poland remain the same as those of former Communist Poland (PRL), established after World War II.

CHAPTER 1

Poland and the Jews
A Historical Survey

Jews were able to live and maneuver in Poland partly because they fitted into the intervening space between two opposing interests within the Polish economy, that of the burghers and that of the nobility. The noblemen demanded free enterprise, in order to promote their newly-organized agricultural estates to the best advantage, and in this they opposed the burghers who maintained monopolized privileges in the economy. Between the two, by exercising considerable tact and agility, the Jew could manage to survive, and even to climb over the economic barriers placed before him.

– Abba Eban, *My People: The Story of the Jews*

The Jews of medieval Europe, suffering from widespread anti-Semitic persecution in the West, found refuge in the East where they were granted religious, economic, and political protection by royal decrees in the Kingdom of Poland. After the Crusades had destroyed the stability of Jewish life in German lands and other parts of Western Europe, Poland became a significant beneficiary as Jewish refugees began pouring into Poland at the invitation of the Polish Kings who, ruling from Poland's capital of *Kraków* (Cracow) until their relocation to the new capital of *Warszawa* (Warsaw) in the early seventeenth century, were eager to apply Jewish capital to the country's development, and to harness Jewish revenues to help

15

them maintain independence from an increasingly hostile Polish nobility.

Since the twelfth century, therefore, Jews prospered as traders and merchants in Polish lands, and many were even put in charge of the mints of the realm. So substantial was the tolerance Jews experienced in medieval Poland that Polish coins occasionally featured the names of princes in Hebrew characters. By the mid-thirteenth century, with their numbers and influence growing, the Jews emerged as the only commercial class in a realm of landlords and peasants.[1] The Jews of Europe, who survived the Crusades, the Inquisition, plagues, countless expulsions, and violent attacks, had been in search of a place where they could lead better lives. They found that place in Poland.

The Benevolence of Poland's Kings

In 1264 Poland's King Bolesław V the Chaste issued a formal "Charter of Jewish Liberties," also known as the Statute of Kalisz, which guaranteed the Jews physical protection, freedom of worship, and autonomy of their religious courts. Therefore, Poland's auspicious climate encouraged an ever-increasing number of Jews to migrate to Poland. Over the ensuing centuries, Jewish immigrants, arriving with extensive business and language skills and vast networks of business connections from their places of origin, made substantial contributions to Poland's economic development.

The charters that protected the rights of Jews were not unique to Poland; they were closely patterned after similar ones granted to Jews in other European lands, the most notable being that conferred[2] in 1244 by Holy Roman Emperor Frederick II. However, those issued in Poland were significant because of their longevity. Whether because of benevolence, personal gain, or a bit of both, Poland's Statute of Kalisz was subsequently ratified by a succession of Polish kings, including Casimir III the Great in 1334—who, in the Statute of Wiślica in 1346, offered the Jews further protection from militant Christians—Casimir IV in 1453, and Sigismund I the Elder in 1539, thus reinforcing official recognition of the Jewish people as a distinct national, religious, linguistic, and cultural group. The civil liberties embodied in these royal decrees were crucial to the flourishing of Jewish life in Poland.

Casimir the Great's additional protections stipulated punitive measures against any town found guilty of anti-Jewish acts; this was just one of many beneficial positions the king initiated during his time in power, for Casimir was indeed one of the most enlightened monarchs of the Middle Ages. Focused on raising the living standards among all classes of his realm, he put politics above war, suppressed the anarchy of the nobility, crafted a famous code of law, promoted commerce, founded the University of Cracow (later bearing the name Jagiellonian University), and built cities, which justifiably earned him the epitaph, "He found a Poland of wood and left behind him a Poland of stone."[3] But Casimir's positive acceptance of the Jews as an essential part of his reconstruction policy proved to be as progressive as it was advantageous for both Poland and the Jewish people in subsequent centuries.

Casimir the Great, last of Poland's Piast dynasty of rulers, left a strong legacy. He made Poland a powerful and influential nation with solid internal organization and positive external relations that prepared Poland to collaborate with other nations, notably Lithuania, in the structure of a common state that would continue for centuries under Jagiellonian rule. The Jagiellonian dynasty, which emerged after Poland's reigning monarch Jadwiga's 1386 marriage to Władysław II Jagiełło, Grand Duke of Lithuania, had profound consequences for Poland's internal composition and national policies. As the last pagan country in Europe, medieval Lithuania changed dramatically after joining Poland, then among Europe's most dynamic and expansive nations. Not only had its pagan religion been quickly abolished, but also within a short period of time everyone except the lowest levels of society became completely Polonized in both language and attitude.[4]

There is no doubt that the greater tolerance enjoyed in the realms of medieval Poland-Lithuania compared to the rest of Europe encouraged further Jewish settlement in Polish-controlled lands, where the Jews were subsequently afforded a system of self-government that permitted jurisdiction over their own religious, cultural, and economic affairs. It comes as no surprise, therefore, that the Jews who began arriving in Poland nearly a millennium ago referred to Poland as *Polin*. Derived from the Hebrew words *po lin*, which according to Jewish tradition implies a place of rest or respite, the term evoked the notion that Poland was a safe place where the oppressed Jews of Europe could find re-

Queen Jadwiga and King Władysław Jagiełło Monument in Cracow, commemorating the 1386 union between Poland and Lithuania.

fuge. Why did the situation change for the worse in subsequent centuries? History reveals the answer.

Wawel Hill

Overlooking the Vistula River, the Royal Castle and Cathedral are situated on Cracow's Wawel Hill, which for centuries served as the residence of Poland's monarchs and as the site of the coronations of kings.

The Jewish Experience in Poland

Long before the horrors of the twentieth century disrupted Jewish life almost irreparably and caused the loss of millions of lives in senseless wars, Poland had been a land of relative peace and opportunity in which Jews from all parts of Europe descended, and where Jewish scholarship flourished for centuries.

In contrast to other Christian rulers of Europe, who took away the rights of Jews and periodically or systematically expelled them, the Polish kings respected the provisions of their medieval agreement with the Jews. This historical fact once made Poland among the most secure places in Europe for the Jews to live. Therefore, Jewish migration to Eastern Europe continued to flow in a steady stream despite Polish society's growing hostility toward the Jews, violent attacks originating from outside the Polish kingdom, and the occasional curtailment of liberties from within.

When the Polish monarchy was strong, Jewish rights were not only acknowledged, but also effectively protected; during a decline protections diminished. After the 1492 death of Casimir IV, the two countries temporarily separated when son John I Albert ascended the throne of Poland, and younger son Alexander became grand duke of Lithuania. Alexander later succeeded his brother as king of Poland after John Albert's premature death in 1501. That same year, the Union of Mielnik reunited Poland and Lithuania. Yet the temporary instability had an effect on the Jews. Between 1495 and 1503 Jews were evicted from Lithuania, and in 1495 the large Jewish community of Cracow, then Poland's capital, was relocated to neighboring Kazimierz. This move was not without a tinge of irony since the district was named for *Kazimierz Wielki*, Poland's benevolent King Casimir the Great.

Despite such occasional setbacks, Poland had indeed remained a refuge for European Jewry, where Jewish intellectual and cultural life thrived and the Jewish population continued to rise. Historians have computed that over the course of the 150-year period from 1501 to 1648, Poland's Jewish population rose from fifty thousand to an astounding half million, during which time strong settlements were established where the Jews were allowed to engage in a wide variety of occupations. Ever since the early sixteenth-century reign of King Sigismund I the Elder, whose passionate Catholic faith did not cloud his vision, Jews were chosen for public service, enabling some

to rise to positions of prominence among those who surrounded the king and his court.[5]

෨෨

There exists a famous tale with support from both
Jewish and Polish sources that symbolizes the political,
economic, and cultural achievements of the Jews in Poland
and the extent to which the leadership of the realm
embraced them. These events revolve around Rabbi Saul
Katzenellenbogen, or Saul Wahl, as he was later known,
who was the reputed "King of Poland" during an interreg-
num for one eventful night in 1587. The story not only
sheds light on Polish legislative anarchy of the sixteenth
century, but also reveals how high some Polish Court Jews
rose within the uppermost circles of the kingdom.[6]

According to legend, Prince Nicholas Radziwill of
Poland-Lithuania, after having been attacked and robbed
in Padua, Italy, met Saul's father, Rabbi Samuel Judah
Katzenellenbogen. Starving and deathly ill, the prince
made his way to the home of the well-known Rabbi
Samuel, who nursed him back to health. In return for his
kindness, Radziwill took with him on his journey back to
Poland a letter for Saul from his father. Upon meeting the
young Saul, who had settled in Poland to further his
Jewish studies after a period of secular studies at the
University of Padua, the Prince, apparently so taken by
Saul's knowledge and integrity, made him his personal
chief advisor in political and commercial affairs.

Saul's illustrious reputation eventually spread among
Poland's nobility, who sought his advice and counsel. In
return, Saul gained leases to Poland's largest salt mines,
which not only brought him great wealth, but also led him
to the court of King Stefan Batory, who admired Saul's
knowledge and abilities. Upon Stefan Batory's death, the

nobles gathered to elect the next king. Because of
competing political factions among the nobles, bribery,
intrigue, and even the attempted intervention of foreign
powers, no king was selected by the appointed deadline of
18 August 1587. Prince Radziwill, understanding that the
fate of Poland was at stake, diffused the situation by rec-
ommending that Saul Katzenellenbogen serve as *rex pro
tempore*, or interim king, until a suitable choice could be
elected.[7] To prevent the prospect of civil war, the Polish
noblemen unanimously agreed to Radziwill's proposal. As
a result, Saul Katzenellenbogen—now known by the surname *Wahl*, Yiddish for "elected"—was reputedly invested
with the full powers of the king. With full rights as
Poland's caretaker king, Saul worked through the night
amending any royal decrees that contained anti-Jewish
provisions. By morning came the election of a new king,
Sigismund III.

Although Saul Wahl's service to Poland as "king for
one night" is recorded as legend, his service to the Polish
monarchy is noted in archival sources. There even exists
a royal decree dated 11 February 1588 by King Sigismund
III describing Saul as having advanced the realm's prosperity. A year later the king wrote more praises about
Saul, conferring upon him a place among royal officials,
thereby granting him the personal protection of Poland's
reigning monarch.

❦

In 1551, King Sigismund II Augustus, Poland's last
ruler of the Jagiellonian dynasty, had issued a proclama-
tion that permitted Jews to elect their own chief rabbi and
judges, answerable only to the king. Justifiably known as
the "Magna Carta" of Jewish self-government, the celebrated charter provided the Jews practical autonomy

within Poland by allowing their own governing agencies, schools, and courts. By this time, Poland's Jewish community had grown large enough to form a well-defined order, like the clergy or the nobility. Hence, it was in keeping with the political philosophy of the day to allow the creation of a "state within a state," for in the absence of an efficient bureaucracy such an arrangement smoothed the process of collecting taxes. By the sixteenth century, therefore, Poland's Jewish communities had achieved a level of autonomy unprecedented in European history when Sigismund II Augustus recognized their right to elect leaders to govern their affairs. The result was a virtually autonomous Jewish state within Poland, giving further justification for the Jews of Poland to regard their host nation as *Polin*, a land of opportunity where they could indeed live safely in exile.

Initially each municipality with a Jewish population had its own *Kahal*, or assembly of elders, who were elected each year during the spring holiday of Passover for a one-year term. The word "Kahal"—signifying community, assembly, or government, with the same meaning as "*Kehillah*"—represented the traditional Jewish form of government in the Diaspora, or the Jewish communities existing outside the biblical land of Israel. In other words, ever since the Jews were compelled to wander from place to place in search of a secure land to live, they had organized their own government so that it would function regardless of what the host governments had set up. Just as in the period of Babylonian captivity in biblical times, in Eastern Europe the Kahal was the power and protectorate to which the religious Jew looked for government and justice. The Kahal issued laws, judged legal cases, and issued divorces to Jews who appealed to the Kahal for distinctly "Jewish" justice rather than appeal to the courts of the land.

The Kahal, having authority over all Jews in each community, even rabbis, was responsible for managing all Jewish communal institutions and collecting their taxes for the kingdom. Regional meetings of exceptional leaders and rabbis of each Kahal took place to settle important legal actions between communities or to pass judgment on appellate cases. By the mid-1500s, however, many of Poland's *Kehillot* (plural of Kahal) were confronting issues that involved Jews in more than one community. Toward the end of the sixteenth century, therefore, another organization had developed out of these meetings, a supreme council that controlled Jewish activities throughout Poland. Led by a group of rabbis and laymen known in Hebrew as *Vaad Arba Aratzot*, or the Council of Four Lands, this powerful national federation governed widely dispersed Jewish communities in the Polish kingdom. By the 1600s there were Jewish settlements in every part of Poland.

The Kingdom of Poland was divided into four provinces: Greater Poland (*Wielkopolska*), with Poznań as its capital, Lesser Poland (*Małopolska*), its capital at Cracow, Red Russia (East Galicia and Podolia), its capital at Lwów, and Volhynia, its capital at Ludmir. A fifth province was added in 1569 when the Principality of Lithuania, with Wilno as its capital, became part of Poland. While Lithuania was initially part of the Council, it separated from the group in 1623 when it obtained its own central organization.

Though all five regions had their own regional associations, the leaders of these groups would periodically gather at the great trading fairs held in Lublin and Jarosław to settle major disputes and discuss issues of common concern. The Vaad Arba Aratzot, or Council of Four Lands, grew out of those meetings and ruled from the mid-1500s to 1764, administering all aspects of Jewish

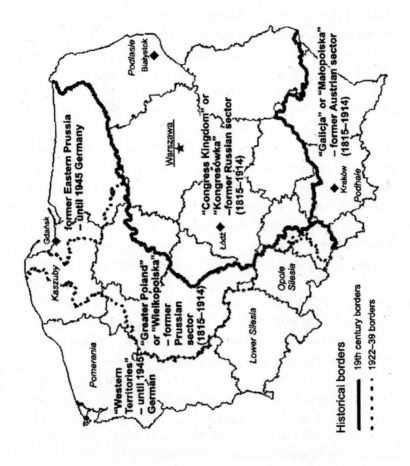

Poland after the eighteenth-century partitions

affairs, from the regulation of religious observances, maintenance of law and order, and adjudication of legal disputes and appeals, to the protection of Polish Jewry's interests at the king's court and Polish parliament, and the collection and distribution of taxes between the districts and the monarchy. It was during this time that Polish scholars of Jewish law and religious commentary, such as Cracow-born Rabbi Moses Isserles (the "Rema"), codifier of Jewish law, and Rabbi Samuel Eliezer Edels (the "Maharsha"), one of the best-known Talmudic commentators, became the leading authorities among world Jewry.

The Polish kingdom had no intention of interfering with the Jewish leadership's authority provided that the Jews continued to pay their taxes to the royal treasury. Indeed, by the mid-eighteenth century, taxes derived from the Jewish community represented a significant proportion of the Polish monarchy's revenues. Therefore, the Council, which acted as the intermediary between the Jews and the Polish authorities, protected Jewish civil interests while it controlled virtually every aspect of life, from the economic, administrative, and fiscal, to the religious, cultural, social, and spiritual, of what had become the greatest Jewish community in the world.

As Poland declined in the eighteenth century so did the Council of Four Lands. Falling into debt, the *Sejm*, or Polish parliament, abolished the Council at the urging of the nobles in 1764, both in Poland and Lithuania, and attempted to increase its income from its Jewish citizens through direct taxation.[8] After central and regional Jewish autonomy was abolished in 1764, only the local autonomy of the Kehillot remained in force, which greatly increased the tax burden of the Jews. The poll tax continued to rise throughout the eighteenth century when even a stamp-tax on Jewish books was imposed.[9]

The Rise and Decline of Jewish Life in Poland

Poland had become a great European power under the Jagiellonian dynasty, whose union with Lithuania led to a "Golden Age" when the Polish-Lithuanian Commonwealth, which ruled from the fourteenth through the sixteenth century, affected all aspects of life and established traditions carried down through the centuries.

Statue of Nicolas Copernicus in Cracow

The Italian Renaissance brought to Poland the humanist spirit of intellectual curiosity, liberal thought, scientific study, and a strong Catholic religious zeal, all of which encouraged native talent in education, science, and literature. Astronomer Nicolas Copernicus, discoverer of the earth's motion around the sun, was a revolutionary product of this time. Later, the Reformation also had a strong impact on Poland with Protestant ideas (particularly of the Swiss Calvinist reformers) attracting a large following among the Polish nobility

Founder of modern astronomy, Nicolas Copernicus (1473–1543) studied astronomy at the Jagiellonian University, where he developed many of his revolutionary theories about the solar system, including the notion that planets orbit around the sun.

with the result that by 1572—the year the Jagiellonian dynasty came to an end—Protestants temporarily held an absolute majority among the lay members of the Senate.[10]

Toward the end of King Sigismund II Augustus's reign, true unification of Poland and Lithuania had finally been achieved by the Union of Lublin in 1569, when one king ruled with a bicameral system of government comprised of bishops and nobles. Hence, the "Silver Age" of the Royal Republic was born. Over the next two hundred years, the Polish-Lithuanian Commonwealth continued to be a haven for refugees from across Europe, including Bohemian Hussites, Dutch Mennonites, and Anabaptists, with the Jewish community continuing to grow.

Since the Jagiellonian era, Poland had been a country that had grown used to a generally peaceful coexistence among Catholicism, Eastern Orthodoxy, Judaism, Protestantism, and even Islam, which made Poland a unique nation in the European continent. While the rest of Europe was being torn apart by religious wars, Poland enacted the Statute of General Toleration in 1573. Although local acts of discrimination and violence could still occur, there was no possibility that a widespread campaign of persecution could break out at that time given the diverse population and progressive policies of the realm. This was a powerful, inclusive period in Poland's history in which the Jewish people prospered.

Between 1569 and 1795 not only had the Polish *szlachta*, or nobility, risen in prominence, but the nature of the monarchy itself also underwent a dramatic transformation as Poland became a "Royal Republic." Following the death of an heirless Sigismund Augustus in 1572, the kings of Poland-Lithuania became an elected body. Hereditary kings were replaced by a system of elected monarchs chosen by an assembly of nobles in the Sejm, and were crowned only after swearing to uphold a long pledge containing articles that guaranteed the principle of toleration; the practice of free elections of the monarch; regular meetings of the Sejm; the nobility's right to declare war and approve taxes and foreign treaties; and the nobility's "Right of Resistance." For its time just prior to the Age of Absolutism in other parts of Europe, this was a radical form of democracy.

Poland's emergence as a *Rzeczpospolita*—a Republic ruled by elected kings—was a momentous historic development since, historian Norman Davies observes, "The noble citizens of the Republic were to be its masters; the king was to be their servant." Indeed, the king of Poland from 1569 until the fateful year of 1795 was less of a limited monarch, like Swedish and English kings, than he was "a manager under contract."[11]

Notwithstanding the advancements of prior generations, by the middle of the seventeenth century the "Silver Age" came to a sudden end when violence reigned and Poland ceased to be a safe haven for Jewish refuge. Not only had the Catholic clergy, a strict and often prejudiced caste, increased its political power base, but Jews, many of whom serving the nobles as tax collectors, financiers, and overseers of their estates, became the targets of popular animosity. This was an unfortunate situation the nobles helped create.

Since nobles were not expected to personally engage in commercial activities—and were even explicitly forbidden from doing so in constitutions of 1633 and 1677—the nobility had developed a "special relationship" with the large Jewish community, particularly in the eastern provinces. There the Jews proved exceedingly useful to noblemen, who could avoid contravening the many regulations that governed economic life in the towns while also prospering from them. Jews were employed as tradesmen, craftsmen, innkeepers, and brokers, deriving favorable interest rates for their efforts. Indeed, many thrived in the service of the great estates of the Polish nobles.[12] The rise of legal privileges among the nobles of Poland occurred virtually at the same time as the rise of serfdom, however, and the nobles insisted on exclusive privileges that effectively gave them supreme power over the lives of serfs tied to their land.[13] Exploited by the nobles, the peasants perceived the Jews as the willing servants of the nobles, whom they hated as much as the oppression itself.

This state of affairs increased the anger of the serfs and therefore contributed to the Jews' precarious position in Poland in the seventeenth century. With the support of the serfs, Ukrainian warrior Bogdan Chmielnicki and his Cossacks had carried out a series of violent uprisings. Not only had he taken out his aggression on Jews but also on Poles, from Catholic priests to the Polish gentry. Villages were pilfered and destroyed. After years of violence, the toll on the Jews of Poland proved enormous. Thousands perished and many Jewish communities were destroyed.

Despite attempts to rebuild from widespread ruin and desolation, more troubles followed. The mutually beneficial relationship between Jews and the Polish monarchs came to an abrupt end after the disappearance of Poland from the political map of Europe—partitioned among the absolute monarchies of Austria, Russia, and Prussia—between 1795 and 1918. With this change, the Jews of Poland lost much of the autonomy they had formerly enjoyed under the rule of the Polish kings. Yet in Austrian-ruled Galicia (Małopolska), which had preserved a strong Polish culture, Jews managed to retain significant rights and freedoms due to the benevolence of Franz Joseph I, Emperor of Austria, who, in the constitution of 21 December 1867, not only removed all preexisting Austrian laws discriminating against Jews, but also forbade the enactment of any harmful anti-Jewish legislation.[14]

In stark contrast to Austria, Jews residing under Russian jurisdiction—the majority—were confined to an area known as the "Pale of Settlement," initiated by

Catherine the Great in 1791, where they were deprived of residential mobility, faced considerable discrimination, and suffered through *pogroms*—violent anti-Jewish attacks. The Jews in Prussia, however, became more culturally assimilated as a result of the effects of the Enlightenment.

Royal Cathedral on Wawel Hill

Considered a masterpiece of Renaissance architecture, the Wawel Cathedral in Cracow with the golden dome of the Sigismund Chapel has great symbolic importance for Polish history and culture. It serves as a mausoleum for many of Poland's kings and houses a treasury of objects commemorating Poland's national glory.

Social upheavals throughout nineteenth-century Europe contributed significantly to the rise of anti-Semitism. Ever since the Industrial Revolution and the corresponding upsurge of a new, powerful working class, the bourgeoisie, deeply disturbed by the developments, found it convenient to focus their neuroses and irrational

fears on the Jews, who thus emerged as the most prominent scapegoat for all of society's ills. Political developments were equally detrimental in this regard. As nationalism grew into a powerful social force, Jews were increasingly viewed as a foreign element among Europe's bur-
geoning nations, with hatred of Jews becoming a leading
expression of national loyalty.

CHAPTER 2

Anti-Semitism in Poland
Nationalist and Communist Influences

*Auschwitz, perhaps the most meaningful symbol of the Holocaust
of the Jewish people, shows to what lengths a system constructed on
principles of racial hatred and greed for power can go. To this day,
Auschwitz does not cease to admonish, reminding us that anti-
Semitism is a great sin against humanity, that all racial hatred
inevitably leads to the trampling of human dignity.*

– Pope John Paul II, *Crossing the Threshold of Hope*

Strong nationalist forces combined with grassroots anti-
Semitic sentiments provided a potent and evil setting for
twentieth-century tragedy. The catastrophe that befell the
Jewish people during the Second World War—with the
most devastating aspects occurring primarily in Nazi-
occupied Poland—was a complex result of fanatical intolerance and unprincipled power. Nazism was the most
extreme example of an abnormal strain of nationalism to
emerge out of the sweltering mix of powerful separatist
processes that had transformed Europe since the nineteenth century. However, nationalism in its various guises
profoundly impacted all parts of Europe, with both positive and negative effects on the general population. The
Jews, a numerically weak minority within a large sea of
European peoples asserting their independence, propelled

by the vigor of self-determination, were burdened by nationalism's more destructive features.

While Poland had been partitioned among the militarily strong, absolute monarchies of Austria, Russia, and Prussia—first in 1772, then again in 1793, and finally in 1795—the Polish national identity was never destroyed. By the end of the nineteenth century, as nationalist sentiments among the subjugated peoples of Europe rose, the national consciousness of Poles had become a particularly formidable force. As a consequence of the First World War and the resurgence of Polish dominance, more than three million Jews found themselves under Polish administration with the 1918 establishment of the independent Second Republic of Poland.

Although the Jews of Poland were ostensibly protected by the minority clauses in the Treaty of Versailles, which guaranteed equal political, legal, and civil rights, as well as control over educational systems, in practice these provisions were not enforced. The Polish government had taken a progressively more severe attitude toward the minorities in general and the Jews in particular, an approach that became especially hostile during the 1930s as a result of domestic developments and the influence of Nazi anti-Semitism. Not only were Jews unjustly blamed for Poland's economic stagnation, but official anti-Jewish policies were expressed in a wide variety of areas, including educational restrictions on the number of Jews admitted to universities, occupational barriers excluding Jews from employment in state-run industries and the civil service, and economic discrimination marked by organized boycotts of Jewish businesses.[1]

In response to the ascent of European nationalism and concurrent rise of anti-Jewish discrimination and persecution in Europe and Russia, Jews in considerable numbers from the late nineteenth century onward became dedicated supporters of Zionism, a Jewish nationalist movement devoted to the establishment of an independent nation for the Jews in the land of their biblical ancestors.

Theodore Herzl, founder of modern political Zionism, emerged in the late nineteenth century as a Jewish personality of great charisma and influence. Herzl's writings and speeches helped rally European Jews around the cause of establishing a Jewish state politically independent of foreign jurisdictions so that Jews could govern themselves and ensure their self-preservation. Yet unlike many European nations that had achieved independence following the First World War—however precarious such independence may have been—the sovereign Jewish State of Israel did not become a reality until the end of the Second World War, after European Jewry had been decimated in the Holocaust.

The Paradox of Polish Communism

The Communist regime that seized control of Poland following the Second World War should have done away with all aspects of anti-Jewish persecution, at least in theory, as classical Communist ideology adhered to the ideal of equality in a classless society. Assimilation was viewed as a natural inevitability, with anti-Semitism, by implication, destined to become a historical footnote.[2]

In conformance with Communism's purported belief in equality, Articles 69 and 70 of Poland's new constitution of 22 July 1952 specifically granted all citizens equality before the law, as well as freedom of conscience and faith, regardless of nationality, religion, or origin.[3] Yet neither Communist doctrine nor Poland's new Soviet-inspired constitution would protect Poles of Jewish extraction from official harassment. In fact, what Poland's

1967–68 "anti-Zionist" campaign conclusively demonstrated was that Marxist ideology was no obstacle preventing Communists from using anti-Semitism as a political weapon. All that was required was another label, a euphemism for anti-Semitism to avoid contravening the ideology.[4] "Anti-Zionism" emerged as one of the most popular brands in 1967.

Perhaps more than any other Eastern European country following the Second World War, Poland was most strongly opposed to the Soviet Union's imposition of Communist rule. With the 1967 Six-Day War as the decisive trigger, therefore, Poland's Communist regime, desperate for support from a public known for its anti-Semitic predilections, unleashed a wide-reaching campaign against Poland's Jews, who through the course of history had become a convenient and common scapegoat for desperate and intolerant regimes.[5]

Political Versus Popular Anti-Semitism

Hatred of Jews, much like hatred of any identifiable group, comes in various forms. But on a fundamental level the hatred of Jews, most popularly known as anti-Semitism, can be viewed as a shared belief among some segments of a population, and as an instrument of terror in the hands of those in power. This distinction is very important due to the powerful effect each has on society.

Political anti-Semitism reflects a political regime's deliberate manipulation and exploitation of popular anti-Semitism to achieve its own agenda. But without the existence of traditional popular anti-Semitic prejudices, the manipulative use of political anti-Semitism would be impossible. Given the implications, political anti-Semitism—particularly when combined with strong grassroots anti-Semitism—represents an even greater threat to the Jewish minority than popular anti-Semitism alone. The reason is simple. When a strategy of persecution is unleashed from the top, the state becomes the oppressor, thereby precluding those targeted from seeking protection from the state. Hitler's Germany was a notorious example.

Considering the impact of anti-Semitism on Poland's 1967–68 domestic policies, an important distinction must be made. In exploring the origins of "popular" anti-Semitism, scholars have pointed to various causes such as the influence of misguided church teachings, xenophobia—an excessive fear of those deemed "foreign"—and the simple resentment of the perceived economic and professional success of some Jews. Polish ignorance of Jewish life, especially of Jewish religious life, helped to reinforce anti-Jewish stereotypes among the general population.[6] Whatever the explanation, popular anti-Semitism has been and continues to be an unpleasant reality of many societies, and unfortunately remains a potent weapon of any regime willing to use it for personal gain. Communist Poland was a prime example.

With regard to "political" anti-Semitism, therefore, whenever a government decides to manipulate a public's predisposition for anti-Jewish sentiments for its own gain, the potential harm to Jews substantially increases. Under such circumstances, Jews in all segments of society become potential targets of oppression, rather than a limited—though no less appalling—number of potential victims of sporadic anti-Semitic outbursts confined to an isolated geographical setting or specific stratum of society. Indeed, Poland's 1967–68 outbreak of domestic political anarchy left Jews powerless to do anything other than try to weather the effects of the political storm initiated and carried out by officials at the highest levels of Poland's government. Because Communist Poland's leadership attempted to manipulate and exploit popular anti-Jewish prejudices on a national scale for its own survival, this book focuses on the political aspect of anti-Semitism rather than the origins of popular anti-Semitism.

Political Anti-Semitism in Communist Poland

Despite the systematic annihilation of European Jewry during the Second World War, carried out mostly on Polish soil under German occupation, postwar Poland was not free of anti-Semitic sentiments. Violent attacks by Poles against Jews indeed occurred. The most infamous of these were the notorious massacres of dozens of Jewish Holocaust survivors in Cracow on 11 August 1945 and Kielce on 4 July 1946.[7] These vicious crimes from the Communist period, carried out by a minority of Poles, seem like minor aberrations when compared to the wartime massacre of 10 July 1941 in the northeastern town of Jedwabne. Soon after Hitler's troops attacked Red Army forces that had occupied eastern Poland under the 1939 Nazi-Soviet Pact, the Jedwabne mass murder was organized and carried out by Catholic Poles against hundreds of their Jewish neighbors. Jews were rounded up and killed in the streets while the rest were herded into a barn and burned alive. Postwar inquiries into the massacre concluded with more than a dozen Poles convicted and imprisoned for the crime.[8]

Rather than deal directly and openly with this most severe form of violent popular anti-Semitism in Poland, the postwar Communist authorities clung to the position that during the Nazi era Poles had always been victims of atrocities, not collaborators or perpetrators of them. This myth was subsequently drawn upon when Poland's Communist regime defended itself against the accusation that anti-Semitism was behind the anti-Zionist campaign of the late 1960s.[9]

Despite such violent examples of anti-Jewish behavior committed by Catholic Poles against Jewish Poles, on the whole the expression of anti-Semitism during the Communist period tended to favor a political form, whereby discrimination against Jews steadily intensified throughout Polish society until reaching its most explosive period between 1967 and 1968. By this time, rather than becoming victims of widespread genocide, influential Poles of Jewish descent were arrested, put on trial, and imprisoned on trumped up charges—a trend all too reminiscent of Stalin's anti-Semitic purges between 1948 and 1953. Though Joseph Stalin's death in 1953 prevented the imminent deportation of most Soviet Jews to Siberia,[10] in the aftermath of the 1967–68 anti-Semitic campaign thousands of Poles of Jewish origin were effectively pushed out of Poland, stripped of their Polish citizenship.

Political anti-Semitism—the intentional misuse of certain long-held popular prejudices against Jews by a political party or movement for its own purposes—was not foreign to Russia, Poland, or other European countries. In the Polish context, however, political anti-Semitism had been a weapon of both *Endecja*, Poland's pre-World War II right-wing National Democratic Party, and Poland's post-World War II ruling Communist Party, which relied upon anti-Jewish prejudices with increasing frequency.[11] Overt political anti-Semitism was therefore not a new phenomenon in Poland when the Communist regime's campaign against Poles of Jewish descent erupted in the late 1960s. What is perplexing, though, is that the use of political anti-Semitism would occur in a nation that, despite formerly having a large, enterprising, and vibrant community of Jewish people, was now virtually absent of Jews.

Prior to the outbreak of the Second World War, Poland had been home to the largest Jewish community in the world, representing about 10 percent of Poland's pre-war general population. During the Holocaust, however, the Nazis murdered three million of Poland's 3.3 million Jews[12]—about 90 percent of Polish Jewry.

Given their desire to leave behind the terrible memories of persecution and rising Polish anti-Semitism, most of Poland's Holocaust survivors emigrated in the years following the war. Likewise, the majority of Polish Jews who survived in the USSR—many died in Soviet labor camps—chose not to resettle in Poland after repatriation from the Soviet Union, preferring instead to immigrate to Israel, North America, or Western Europe.[13] As a result, by the late 1950s, there were roughly thirty to forty thousand Poles of Jewish origin remaining in Poland—a mere 1 percent of their prewar population.[14] By 1967, the number of Poles of Jewish descent still residing in Poland had declined even further. At that time, the number of Jews ranged from twenty-five to thirty thousand, constituting less than 0.1 percent of Poland's general population of more than thirty-one million.[15]

In view of the numerical, political, and economic weakness of the Jewish ethnic group in post-Stalinist Poland, the intensity and scope of the 1967–68 anti-Semitic campaign proved truly astonishing. Considering Poland's miniscule Jewish population, the underlying reasons for the harassment of Jews initiated and carried out by key members of Poland's leadership are as puzzling as they are shameful.

∽

By the late 1960s, Władysław Gomułka, first secretary of the ruling Communist Polish United Workers' Party (PUWP), was struggling to maintain control over his party and, in turn, ensure his party's control over the nation. Following the "Polish October" of 1956 that returned him to power, Gomułka, in line with the trend throughout the Communist world, had asserted that there were "many roads to Socialism" and therefore transformed Poland into a "client state" of the Soviet Union rather than the "puppet state" Poland had been under the pro-Stalinist leadership of Bolesław Bierut.[16]

The "Polish October" introduced what on the surface appeared to be an anti-Soviet regime in Poland. But because no outbreak of violence was involved, it was the Hungarian Revolution, which erupted during the same period, that captured the world's attention. The relatively silent (though decisive) events taking place in Poland were overlooked. Despite October 1956, over the next ten years Gomułka's unfulfilled promises of liberalization and further cultural repressions contributed to widespread public dissatisfaction with Poland's Soviet-sponsored Communist government and its cultural, economic, and political policies.

Heightened discontent led to the eruption of a national crisis following the government's abrupt cancellation on 30 January 1968—for alleged anti-Soviet overtones— of Warsaw's National Theater production of D*ziady (Forefathers' Eve)*, an anti-Tsarist nineteenth-century historic drama. Its author, patriot Adam Mickiewicz, had long been regarded not only as the greatest Polish poet, but also as one of the greatest Slavic poets. Throughout the month of March, demonstrations took place on university campuses across Poland condemning domestic censorship, violent police tactics, and biased press reports.

The government's extreme reaction against both real and fabricated opponents of Poland's Soviet-imposed Communist regime revealed an intolerance and fear of an unchecked rise in popular discontent, while also reflecting internal rivalries within the leadership of the PUWP. Evidence further suggests that by pinning blame on a traditional scapegoat for problems affecting contemporary Poland, the government's heavy-handed response served as a "deliberate provocation" whose purpose was to reassert the dominance of the Communist Party.[17]

While Polish authorities carried out mass arrests of alleged agitators, including more than two thousand students and numerous eminent figures among the intelligentsia, the government's oppressive response featured the dramatic acceleration and intensification of an overt, government-initiated policy of anti-Semitism that began the prior year. With Gomułka's leadership position under threat, especially by Interior Minister General Mieczysław Moczar, political anti-Semitism had become a powerful instrument of manipulation following the Arab-Israeli War of June 1967, both within the PUWP and throughout Polish society.

Moczar relied on the support of an increasingly influential organization that he led—*Związek Bojowników o Wolność i Demokrację (ZBoWiD)*, the Union of Fighters for Freedom and Democracy. Comprised of veterans and members of the underground resistance, this organization was ideologically situated within the sphere of the so-called Partisan faction of the Party, which, despite the name, did not reflect the wide assortment of wartime resistance groups of partisans who had fought against the Nazi occupation. Causes for its transparent policy of political anti-Semitism were as complex as the effects were devastating, both to Polish Jewry's long history and to Polish society itself.

Situated in Cracow's Market Square (Rynek Główny), among the largest town squares in Europe, stands the statue of poet and playwright Adam Mickiewicz (1798–1855), whose writings epitomized Polish patriotism. The statue is surrounded by allegorical figures representing the nation, education, poetry, and courage.

Władysław Gomułka, First
Secretary of the Communist
Polish United Workers' Party

© *Hulton-Deutsch Collection/*
CORBIS/MAGMA

Interior Minister General
Mieczysław Moczar

© *Bettmann/CORBIS/MAGMA*

CHAPTER 3

The 1967 Middle East Crisis
Soviet Policy and Poland's Response

The United States and Britain may have felt a little uneasy about their courtship of Nasser's Egypt, but the Soviet Union had no qualms at all. The fact that the USSR was making possible the fulfillment of the Egyptian dream of a second round of war against Israel was justified—to the extent that the Russians ever feel that they have to justify themselves—on the grounds that Zionism, which was such an evil thing, had to be suppressed everywhere.

– Golda Meir, *My Life*

On 5 June 1967, Israel, confronted by the imminent threat of a united Arab military offensive led by Egypt's president Gamal Abdel Nasser—Israel's most vocal enemy in the region—launched a devastating preemptive strike that resulted in the swift destruction of the Egyptian air force, accompanied by equally effective ground battles against Egypt, Jordan, and Syria. The Six-Day War concluded on 10 June 1967, with Israel in control of the entire Sinai Peninsula in Egypt, all Jordanian territory west of the Jordan River, and the strategic Golan Heights of Syria. While Israel's decisive victory over the well-armed and substantially larger Arab force increased Jewish pride around the world, the enormity of the Arab defeat not only embarrassed Nasser and his Arab allies, but also humiliated the Soviet Union, which had been the chief military advisor and arms provider of Egypt and Syria.

The Soviet Union, having branded Israel as the aggressor in the conflict, cut off diplomatic relations with the Jewish state on 10 June 1967. Rather than focus its public rhetoric against the Jewish people directly, however, the Soviet regime vilified "Zionism" and "Zionists" in its intensive barrage of radio and press reports.[1] Labeled "Zionist sympathizers," Jews were easy targets for exploitation and persecution. As subsequent reports confirmed, many Soviet citizens and students had indeed been arrested and charged with the "crime" of Zionism.[2] By directing its propaganda campaign against the "evils" of Zionism, therefore, the leadership of the Union of Soviet Socialist Republics could deny Western accusations of anti-Semitism. In fact, Soviet authorities had always officially denied that anti-Semitism or any kind of prejudice existed in the USSR, citing the Soviet constitution's guarantees of complete equality for all Soviet citizens.[3] Given the USSR's considerable influence over the foreign policies of Soviet satellite states like Poland, as well as other Communist regimes dependent on Soviet support, broad condemnation of Zionism and the State of Israel's role in the Six-Day War was virtually assured.

Poland's Reaction to the Six-Day War

Contrary to the Polish government's official position on Israel's victory, popular reaction among Poles was overwhelmingly pro-Israel. Not only did Poles perceive the Arab defeat as a defeat of the Soviets, the Arab nations' main benefactor, but they also saw Israel's victory as Poland's victory, since Polish Jews had dominated the military force that defeated the Soviet-sponsored Arabs.[4] Rather than signifying a profound concern for the Jewish people, however, Poland's favorable public opinion toward Israel likely had more to do with the Poles' hatred of the oppressive Soviet regime, a prospect which helps explain the Polish government's markedly different response.

Having recognized the importance of maintaining good Polish-Soviet relations to repel any future German-led aggression and prevent any further Soviet intervention in Poland's domestic affairs, Poland's Communist regime had closely followed all aspects of Soviet foreign policy and its "anti-imperialist" crusade against the Western democracies. Poland severed diplomatic relations with Israel on 12 June 1967. But what ignited flames was Władysław Gomułka's ominous speech before the Sixth Congress of the Central Council of Polish Trade Unions on 19 June 1967, alleging that a dangerous "Zionist Fifth Column" existed in Poland.

In this widely publicized tirade, Gomułka singled out Poles of Jewish origin as instigators of an anti-Soviet campaign, agents of Western imperialism, and propagators of an aggressive brand of Zionism.[5] From this moment on, the Polish government embarked upon one of the most severe anti-Semitic campaigns of the postwar era, a vicious crusade that resulted in the expulsion and emigration of over half of the remaining Jewish population.[6] So ferocious was the rhetoric emanating from the highest echelons of the Polish leadership that even Yugoslavia's Marshal Tito, considered the oldest and staunchest friend of Nasser in Eastern Europe, publicly rebuked Poland's anti-Zionist rhetoric.

Although domestic popular opinion favoring Israel may have prompted an embarrassed Polish regime to lash out at anyone sympathetic to Israel's plight during the Six-Day War—proving how ineffective two decades of anti-Western and pro-Soviet propaganda had been in Poland—this alone fails to account for the viciousness of the subsequent domestic campaign against Poland's Jews. First, not every Soviet-allied nation complied with the Soviet Union's official line. For example, Romania, rather than break its ties with Israel, blamed Arab leaders for refusing to recognize Israel's right to exist and urged negotiations between the opposing parties. Cuba, another faithful Communist regime, did not break its ties with Israel. Second, among Communist nations that censured Israel—either to conform to official Soviet policy or to serve their own domestic and international policy concerns—most reserved their condemnatory political rhetoric for "aggressive" Zionism rather than Israel's Jewish citizens, or, more critically, the Jewish populations that continued to reside in Communist Eastern Europe. For instance, neither Hungary nor Yugoslavia, despite prior histories of anti-Semitic policies and the continued presence of sizeable Jewish communities, displayed any open anti-Semitism at this time. In stark contrast to most Communist regimes of the Soviet orbit, therefore, Poland's official reaction did not cease with its condemnation of Israel, but assumed a seemingly irrational domestic campaign of official anti-Semitism under the pretext of anti-Zionism.

Polish Nationalism and Political Anti-Semitism

Though Russian and European nationalism had historically been a powerful impetus for the rise of popular anti-Semitism, neither Poland's strong nationalism nor popular anti-Semitism is sufficient to account for the program of political anti-Semitism that Poland's leadership pursued following the Six-Day War. Comparing the official reactions of Poland and Romania—two former Communist nations that share a long tradition of "folk" anti-Semitism and very marked nationalism—is particularly revealing.

While Poland's Jewish population was only about twenty-five thousand in 1967, Romania not only had more than three times Poland's number, but the Romanian Jewish community enjoyed considerable cultural and religious freedoms. Eastern European nationalism cannot automatically be equated with anti-Semitism, therefore, especially not of the political variety. The different reactions among the Soviet satellites had more to do with the degree of each country's relative freedom from Soviet control and the relative receptiveness to anti-Semitic policies. Romania's ability to maintain cordial relations with Israel was primarily due to the Communist nation's considerable degree of independence within the Soviet Bloc. In Poland direct Soviet influence was much greater, and therefore extensive anti-Semitism persisted even though very few Jews had remained in Poland by the late 1960s.[7]

Not only had Polish Jews with strong Zionist sympathies chosen to immigrate to Israel shortly after the war, followed by a second wave of emigration in 1956–57, but Poland's Communist government had abolished all non-Communist-controlled Jewish organizations as far back as 1948. Not only had Poland banned Zionist parties, but all Jewish schools had also been nationalized, and the teaching of Hebrew—deemed a "national" language for its official status in Israel—was practically eliminated.[8] By 1966, although there were five schools where Yiddish was still taught in Poland, a principal in Wrocław, one of the more important centers of Jewish life in postwar Poland, complained that his students spoke only Polish at home. This underscores the considerable assimilation occurring in postwar Poland.[9]

Taking into consideration postwar Jewish emigration, state-imposed restrictive measures on Jewish life, and rapid assimilation of Jews into mainstream Polish society, no legitimate domestic Zionist "threat" existed in Poland at the time of the Six-Day War. A Jew who wished to leave Poland for Israel had been permitted to do so since 1956. Thus, logic dictates that by 1968, any Jew who had chosen to remain in Poland was, as British political writer Nicholas Bethell asserts, "surely a Pole first and a Jew second, and therefore not a Zionist,"[10] certainly not if the implication meant harboring sentiments against the Polish state.

Numerous Poles of Jewish and non-Jewish extraction felt justifiable sympathy for Israel in 1967. In fact, the commander of the Polish air force and two other senior officers were removed from their positions for refusing to keep the Party's anti-Israel position. Poland's domestic response against the small Jewish minority obviously had more complex influences than just staunch nationalism or strong popular anti-Semitism, particularly since Poland lacked any organized Zionist movement that could have served as a true potential threat to the state.

❧

After the Second World War, Russian anti-Semitism had both been forced upon the Soviet satellites and voluntarily copied by them, which ultimately rebounded in more anti-Jewish measures in the Soviet Union. In terms of government policy, this meant that anti-Semitism flowed from the USSR westward and, after being reinforced in the satellites, returned to the USSR. Therefore, rather than adhere to the Communist ideals of "internationalism" and "brotherhood," anti-Semitism and the near globalization of anti-Zionism had come to flourish in the Soviet Union.[11]

Since anti-Zionist and anti-Jewish policies were championed by Stalin, and pursued with almost as much vigor by Nikita Khrushchev and his successor Leonid Brezhnev, Soviet influence over Poland's Jewish policy cannot be ignored. While the leadership of Poland's Communist Party must certainly bear primary responsibility for what ensued in Poland under its direction, Soviet anti-Zionist and anti-Jewish policies—whether explicitly dictated by the Kremlin or implicitly by Soviet example—contributed to Poland's anti-Semitic campaign. Before examining the particulars of Poland's 1967–68 domestic campaign, therefore, a review of Soviet policy toward the Middle East, Zionism, and Soviet Jews is necessary to assess how the USSR influenced Poland's international and domestic political decisions regarding Israel and Poland's own Jewish population.

Soviet Strategy in the Middle East

Despite Lenin and Stalin's consistent opposition to Zionism, by 1947 the Soviet Union defended the establishment of a Jewish state in part of Palestine, and was even among the first countries to recognize the State of Israel's momentous May 1948 Declaration of Independence. Andrei Gromyko, then Soviet Ambassador to the United Nations, had given numerous impassioned speeches between 1947 and 1948 in support of Israel. Stalin's decision to support the establishment of a Jewish state in British-controlled Palestine was strategic, however, since it provided an opportunity to not only reduce Great Britain's influence in the region, but also to establish a Russian base in Israel during the Cold War.[12]

After Israel had emerged triumphant in its War of Independence, effectively removing the British from the region, Soviet support for Israel quickly waned. Again, Soviet political strategy was at work. In its Cold War battle against the United States for world influence, the

USSR, well aware of the pro-West orientation of Israel's ruling socialist Zionist party *Mapai*, abandoned its pro-Israel position to pursue stronger relations with the Arab states—at Israel's expense. In most Arab countries during the early 1950s, when Communist parties were either outlawed or in their early stages of development, the Soviet Union focused its attention on the needs of these nations. After Premier Georgy Malenkov's speech before the Supreme Soviet on 8 August 1953, which made friendly overtures to Middle Eastern governments, Egypt was among the first to make positive references to Soviet foreign policy.

Soviet involvement in the region intensified significantly, however, when Khrushchev decided to sell arms to Egypt and Syria in response to the 1955 signing among countries near the Soviet frontier—Iraq, Turkey, Pakistan, and Iran—of the pro-Western "Baghdad Pact." This military alliance was supported by Great Britain, still an acknowledged world power and founding member of NATO. Although considered an appropriate defensive measure by Western nations, the Soviet government regarded the Pact as a potential threat to its security.

Ensuring that Egypt and other Arab nations became increasingly dependent on Moscow, the Soviet Union continually enlarged its military aid. Nasser, who quickly emerged as the leader of Arab opposition to Israel's existence, therefore obtained a huge arsenal of Soviet weapons to support his dubious cause to eliminate Israel. In response to the 1967 dramatic defeat of its Arab clients, a humiliated USSR redoubled its shipment of modern armaments to Egypt and Syria while going on the diplomatic offensive to coerce Israel to retreat unconditionally to its prewar borders. Domestic and international strategy was at the root of these actions. Not only did the USSR wish to remain a superpower, appease the hawks in its politburo, and impede America's strategy of global supremacy, but there was also a fervent belief that the Soviet Empire should be broadened to include the Arab nations in order to serve as a massive bloc against the West. On the other hand, the doves of the politburo, who preferred to focus on improving society and the Soviet economy rather than pursue grand territorial ambitions abroad, considered the feverish pro-Arab, anti-Israel position as a distasteful necessity in order to avoid the sudden collapse of the USSR's international position.

Umberto Terracini, co-founder of the Italian Communist Party, believed that Soviet tactics revealed "a complete absence of moral considerations in the Soviet Union's foreign policy decisions," since the very ideological principles the USSR had proclaimed to follow were sacrificed. In Terracini's view, Soviet hypocrisy was most apparent in the Soviet regime's cultivation of strong relations with the Arab nations, "which after their liberation from colonial domination, established political institutions and economic systems having absolutely nothing to do with socialism." These were autocratic regimes with immense wealth from oil resources that belonged exclusively to whoever happened to hold political power.[13]

Rather than serve as a reflection of authentic ideological or socioeconomic concerns, therefore, Soviet favoritism of the Arab nations over Israel was primarily based on strategic interests.[14] Soviet Jewry, however, served as an equally significant domestic factor in the development of Soviet foreign policy.

Soviet and Polish Exploitation of the Jews

The Soviet Union's change in strategy from supporting Israel to supporting Arab regimes can also be attributed to the growth of Soviet Jewry's identification with the

State of Israel. A consistent feature of totalitarian regimes like the USSR is the desire to secure complete uniformity among the population: the more homogenous the population, the better the chances of the regime to survive and strengthen its rule.[15] However, after Israel asserted its independence, many Jews, inspired by the Soviet government's apparent sympathetic attitude toward the struggling Jewish state, felt that they might be able to go to Israel and help defend it. Demonstrating their enthusiasm, fifty thousand Soviet Jews came to Moscow's central synagogue on 16 October 1948 to greet Golda Meir, Israel's first ambassador to the USSR. The Soviet leadership considered this public event to be an intolerable breakdown of its policy.

In the totalitarian regime of the USSR, there was no acceptance of the idea that the Soviet Jewish community belonged both to the Jewish people throughout the world and, on a sentimental level, to the new State of Israel. A reflection of the seriousness of the Soviet position, Stalin even ordered the arrest of those Jews who could be identified from photos taken at the Moscow event.[16] While the renewed bond between Soviet Jewry and Israel significantly deepened Soviet antagonism toward the Jews and Zionism, this hostility, present since Tsarist times, had thrived under the Soviet regime. Not confined to the Soviet Union, however, such sentiments were embraced and used in Poland's anti-Jewish campaign.

The establishment of Israel as a pro-Western independent Jewish state in the Near East, and the development of a close relationship between the USSR and the Arab nations, heightened official Soviet hostility toward Jews under the pretext of anti-Zionism and opposition to the West. Moreover, the spread of Soviet anti-Jewish sentiments and policies into Soviet-supported Eastern European Communist administrations set the stage for the implementation of official anti-Semitism, particularly in Poland, which had a large patriotic population opposed to Soviet domination of a Polish nation under pressure. Israel's victory during the Six-Day War, therefore, provided a convenient excuse for a beleaguered Polish Communist Party to exploit a favorite scapegoat—Jews—by implementing a sweeping campaign of anti-Semitism while appearing to conform to the Soviet Union's official "anti-Zionist" position against Israel. Indeed, the volatile combination of Russian and Soviet anti-Jewish policies, Soviet Middle-East policy, and the immediate events of the Six-Day War, helped foster a climate that made Poland's 1967–68 anti-Semitic campaign possible.

Before exploring the kind of anti-Semitism that was fostered by the Soviet regime, the campaign of domestic terror that took place in Poland in 1967–68 shall first be examined together with an analysis of why Jews tend to assume the burden for regimes in search of someone to blame, even if blame has to be manufactured.

CHAPTER 4

Poland's Assault
on the Jews, 1967–68
A Contrived Solution for Social Dissent

History teaches that virulent smear campaigns do not always lead to the extreme of genocide, but without such campaigns the latter would be impossible. This makes the systematic incitement of hatred against any minority so dangerous and its consequences so unpredictable.

– Josef Banas, *The Scapegoats: The Exodus of the Remnants of Polish Jewry*

Although Poland was among the Soviet Union's preeminent postwar allies, by the 1960s a significant segment of Poland's population had grown increasingly hostile to Władysław Gomułka's Communist regime and the Soviet Union's effective control of Poland. The younger generation, which as a percentage of the total population had grown substantially since the end of the war, emerged as a potent force against the government's poor economic planning and cultural repression. Likewise, as a result of factional divisions within the PUWP, the "Partisans" led by Interior Minister Mieczysław Moczar had become a formidable destabilizing force that threatened Gomułka's authority over Poland and the Communist Party. In the eyes of the Kremlin leadership, both of these factors could have caused doubts about the reliability of Gomułka's government.

Clamping down on growing signs of public discontent, Gomułka sought to pacify Soviet authorities and repel the various threats to his leadership by carrying out a policy—popular among the rival Partisans—that tinged of desperation. Since Poland was a nationalist hotbed of anti-Semitism, an official anti-Semitic policy—thinly veiled under the guise of Soviet-sanctioned anti-Zionism—emerged as a seemingly natural though inherently evil course of action.

Given Poland's social instability under Communist rule, the main sources of anti-government feelings are first considered, followed by an analysis of a Polish government policy that thinly masked officially sanctioned political anti-Semitism. Assessing motives for the Communist regime's anti-Semitic rhetoric and actions, attention is directed to Poland's specific sociopolitical challenge—the emergence of a large youthful demographic—and the ascent of Moczar, whose influence over Gomułka and Poland's Communist establishment fueled the domestic attack on Jews and intellectuals between 1967 and 1968.

Poland's Failing Economic and Cultural Policies

When Gomułka assumed the political leadership of Poland in 1956, he demonstrated skills as an articulate reformer who promised Poles economic improvements, increased freedoms, and greater independence from the Soviet Union. Consequently, Gomułka's rise to power was accompanied by considerable popular support. By the 1960s, however, it had become clear that Gomułka's domestic and foreign policies had not evolved in the direction that many had hoped and expected. In the opinion of many Poles, Gomułka's policies led to stagnation in Poland and unquestioning subordination to the Soviet Union in foreign relations. Not only had Gomułka failed to implement effective economic reforms, but he also failed to increase Poland's autonomy from the Soviet Union. As if to compensate for his weakening position at home, Gomułka had moved closer to Moscow by siding with the Kremlin in its disputes with Romania, Czechoslovakia, and, in 1967, the Middle East.

Gomułka's retreat from the promises of 1956 was partly due to the changing balance of forces in the Communist world. By 1957, after the Hungarian uprising had been suppressed, Gomułka found himself isolated since, except for Yugoslavia, the remaining Eastern European countries were either suspicious of him because of his lack of ideological orthodoxy, or jealous of his autonomy.[1] This jealousy had quickly arisen following Gomułka's 1956 return to power. As the old Stalinist system of direct Soviet rule over the satellites had become less viable, Khrushchev, recognizing that Gomułka was among the very few Polish politicians capable of binding Poland closer to Moscow, removed many Soviet "advisers" from Poland and reduced the visibility of Red Army troops within the Polish borders to reinforce the image of an enhanced Polish autonomy.

Despite his precarious position within the Communist bloc, Gomułka had begun liberalizing Poland's former Stalinist totalitarian system. As part of his policy, Gomułka loosened labor discipline. The effects of this measure were sporadic strikes and work stoppages from the end of 1956 through 1957. As a consequence, Gomułka's actions ultimately proved detrimental to his popularity, as he undermined the pressure that had kept the old economic system functioning before revived individual initiative and material and moral labor incentives had a chance to successfully stimulate the Polish economy.[2] Popular anger continued to ferment as the economy worsened and increasingly repressive measures were introduced to restore order.

Although Polish economic history is complex, it is fair to say that government action, and inaction, enraged many Poles. In 1967, for example, several months prior to the start of the anti-Semitic campaign, Gomułka had promised that Polish industrial output would yield larger quantities of higher-quality consumer products with an improved distribution system. What actually materialized were long lines of people seeking meat, vegetables, fruit, and winter clothing at retail shops, while state warehouses were overstocked with goods that could not be sold since they were either priced too high or were of inferior quality. Moreover, prior to Christmas 1967, the government raised the price of meat by 30 percent after the prices for gas, electricity, coal, milk, fish, cigarettes, transportation, and housing had recently been raised.[3]

Such examples lead to one incontrovertible fact: the popularity of Gomułka and his government could only decline as a result of poorly designed, ineffective, and clearly unpopular domestic policy initiatives. Rather than accept old excuses as causes for the present economic difficulties—such as damaged infrastructure from the war, or the incompetence of factory and managerial talent in the agricultural sector—Poles more logically attributed the responsibility to the incompetent administration and the Communist system itself. After all, with such an apparently inept leadership running the nation, why should the population find favor with the existing regime?

As economic troubles and cultural repression continued to rise, dissatisfaction with Gomułka's regime turned into open defiance by the "Polish intelligentsia," a class of educated people that included scholars, teachers, physicians, lawyers, writers, and artists who earned their livelihoods from their knowledge and skills.[4] In March 1964, in a protest letter delivered to the Polish government, thirty-four highly respected academics clearly conveyed their disapproval of the regime's increasing restrictions on freedom of expression; in 1966, during a lecture at Warsaw University, prominent philosopher Professor Leszek Kołakowski criticized Gomułka's government's ten years of regressive policies; and on 29 February 1968 the Warsaw branch of the Writers' Union vigorously protested against the government's ban of Mickiewicz's play, *Dziady*. Furthermore, when the voices of discontent among the intellectuals expanded to include students, the government greeted their outbursts with severe reprisals. Many academics, writers, and students were harassed, dismissed from their positions, and, in many notable cases, arrested. Although Kołakowski was expelled from the Communist Party and lost his university chair as punishment for his public lecture critical of the regime—and his prior criticisms of the government's suppression of dissent—his example only strengthened the opposition's resolve.

Protests of March 1968: The Opposition of Poland's Youth

Despite being born, raised, and educated under the rule of Communism, Poland's rebellious youth was a significant potential threat to the Communist regime. After the Communists came to power, while many students joined officially sanctioned Communist student organizations, a substantial number of students, particularly those who were opposed to Communism and supporters of the Catholic Church, did not become members. Such defiance of the dictates of the regime escalated in the 1960s when a strong protest movement emerged.

Two young Warsaw University instructors, Karol Modzelewski and Jacek Kuroń, had influenced a new generation of Polish students into active criticism of Communist institutions in their 1965 "Open Letter to the Party," which was highly critical of the repressive Communist bureaucracy. Arrested and imprisoned for their actions, and supported by writers and liberal-minded professors who joined in the effort to abolish censorship and achieve greater cultural freedoms, Kuroń and Modzelewski inspired students to do the same. In March 1968, the students' pent-up frustrations finally erupted across Poland's university campuses.

When Warsaw University students Adam Michnik and Henryk Szlajfer were expelled on 4 March 1968 for their involvement in the protest following *Dziady's* closure, a series of student-led demonstrations broke out throughout the month on university campuses across Poland—first in Warsaw, then Cracow, Poznań, Lublin, and other cities. Although personal interests, values, and goals among urban and rural youth may have differed, Poland's 350 thousand college students, regardless of origin, were at the front line of the youth movement, demonstrating considerable organizational abilities and politicization that other youths lacked.[5] After the first demonstration took place in Warsaw on 8 March 1968, protests went on for three weeks. Tens of thousands of university students and adult sympathizers rallied on campuses throughout Poland. Beaten with nightsticks by militia forces sent in to quell the demonstrations, thousands were arrested.

The pretext for these student uprisings occurred on 30 January 1968, when the Polish government suddenly banned performances by the National Theater in Warsaw

Warsaw University

The partition of Poland among the Russian, Prussian, and Austrian powers in the late 1700s separated Warsaw from Poland's historic academic center in Cracow, which led Alexander I, Emperor of Russia and King of Poland, to grant permission for the establishment of Warsaw University in 1816.

of *Dziady,* an epic drama about the Polish people's struggle for freedom against early nineteenth-century Russian oppression. Many Poles viewed this as a symbolic act of cultural terrorism. Not only had Polish nationalist feelings been deeply offended but, as former director of Polish Broadcasting for Radio Free Europe Jan Nowak also observes, "Public opinion interpreted the move as evidence of Gomułka's growing servility to the Russian 'big brother.'"[6] Reports suggested that Polish officials were upset about audiences applauding in the "wrong" places, especially during passages that spoke of Polish suffering under Russian rule.[7]

During the March demonstrations, not only did students demand the reinstatement of Michnik and Szlajfer, but they also appealed for the abolition of censorship and called on the government to respect the constitutional guarantees of freedom of speech and civil rights. After all, article 71 paragraph 1 of Poland's constitution guaranteed free speech, free press, and the freedom of meetings, assemblies, processions, and demonstrations. Hence, while students at the Jagiellonian University were adopting a resolution calling for the regime to respect the constitution, over a dozen students in Warsaw—led by former lecturer and outspoken critic of the regime, Jacek Kuroń—put forth a resolution demanding Michnik and Szlajfer's immediate readmission on the grounds that their expulsion had been illegal.[8]

Polish students had never been reluctant to assert their views, and "March 1968" was therefore not the first display of discontent among students in Poland. Given centuries of autonomy enjoyed by Polish universities—particularly at Cracow's Jagiellonian University—it was no surprise that the Nazis, just after occupying Poland during the Second World War, had quickly shut down Poland's universities and sent professors to concentration camps. Independent thought had been vigorously opposed by both Fascist and Communist regimes.[9]

Notwithstanding the similarities shared with prior generations of rebellious students, particularly a predisposition to assert strong and often vocal autonomous views, the students' actions of 1968 underscored the growing power of Poland's youth and also confirmed the significant generation gap that had emerged in Communist Poland between the ruling party and the general population. By the mid-1960s, Poland's population below age thirty-five represented 66 percent of the population while the average age of Politburo members was about sixty.[10]

Since younger people tend to be more receptive to change—in stark contrast to the goals of a repressive Communist regime comprised of an older leadership intent on maintaining the status quo—conflict is virtually inevitable. Nonetheless, the students' demands were moderate and reasonable.

Jagiellonian University

In 1364, King Casimir the Great received permission from the Pope to establish a university in Cracow, the capital of the Kingdom of Poland. Later named Jagiellonian to commemorate the dynasty of Polish kings, it was the second university founded in Central Europe, after Prague in 1348.

During their demonstrations, students did not attack Communism or the Soviet Union, nor did they express support of America and the West. Moreover, there was no criticism directed against Gomułka and the party leadership. Rather, student slogans across the nation repeatedly called for freedom of speech, freedom of assembly, freedom of scientific research, and respect for civil rights pledged by the constitution. There were also demands for an end to government-initiated reprisals, cries for the release of imprisoned protesters, and calls for respect for truth in public media. The expanding campaign of anti-Semitism that had begun nine months earlier was denounced. Thus, besides confirming the growing power of Poland's youth and ever-widening generation gap, "March 1968" also represented the final collapse of all the surviving forms of liberalism that people had misguidedly associated with Gomułka's return to power in 1956.

Although Poland's large younger generation represented a wide range of political views, only a small proportion—less than 5 percent of Cracow university students, for example—had belonged to the Communist Party. Of those who did belong, most tended to be critical of Gomułka's leadership for its ineffective economic plans and repressive cultural policies.[11] In a survey of students at Warsaw University in 1958, only 13 percent considered themselves Marxists; replicated twenty years later, the survey suggested only a slight rise to 18 percent. While a variety of factors contributed to these numbers, the relatively few self-declared Marxists underscored the popularity among Poland's youth of the culture, values, fashions, and ways of thinking dominant in Western Europe and the United States.[12]

The greater freedoms and democracy that young Poles were demanding on university campuses in March 1968 were not possible in Poland without angering Soviet authorities and encouraging potential Soviet military intervention, as the Prague Spring would soon confirm. The Soviet Union desired docile, subordinate, and loyal regimes along its borders, which Gomułka undoubtedly understood given the accommodation he had negotiated with the Soviet leadership when he came to power during the "Polish October" of 1956. At that momentous time in Poland's postwar Communist history, Gomułka successfully argued Poland's case to follow its own path to socialism in return for continued subservience to the Soviet Union, a position to which Khrushchev agreed. This transformed the Polish People's Republic from being a "puppet state" of the USSR to a "client state."[13]

In 1968, however, besides ignoring the students' legitimate concerns, the government deliberately made the situation worse by deploying specially equipped police and militia units to attack unarmed demonstrators.[14] Concurrently, a propaganda campaign was carried out through the media that vilified protesting intellectuals, students, and, above all, Jews. Poland's Jews were put in deliberate danger, therefore, as a result of the regime's furious attempt to maintain and enhance its power. The Jews had indeed become a perfect target for Poland's Communist leadership.

Polish Jews—A Convenient Scapegoat

Throughout history, the term "scapegoat" has been symbolic for people blamed or punished for the wrongdoings of others. This has not always been a metaphor, but was originally based on an ancient sacred ritual outlined in Leviticus, chapter 16. According to biblical law, on the holiest day of the Jewish year, Yom Kippur (the Day of Atonement), two male goats were to be brought to the altar of the Tabernacle. The High Priest would choose one of them at random for immediate sacrifice while the other was sent off into the wilderness and permitted to escape. The latter goat symbolically carried with it all the sins of the people. Hence, this ancient rite still survives to this day in the common expression *scapegoat*. "But the omission of a single letter, which once prefixed the word," notes scholar of origins Rudolph Brasch, "hides its original meaning. The escaped goat became the scapegoat!"[15] Thus, Jews, numerically weak and often the object of scorn by those more powerful in European society and elsewhere, had often been compelled to assume this unfortunate role. In the late 1960s, the Jews of Poland were again the principal example of this shameful trend.

In the early 1960s, rising discontent among workers and intellectuals contributed to the emergence of a power struggle amid contesting groups of Communists vying for power over the Polish Communist Party. Consequently, the PUWP, unable to solve Poland's economic problems with Gomułka at the helm, had splintered among three rival groups. Gomułka represented the centrist and moderate faction. He faced challenges from the so-called Technocrats led by Politburo member Edward Gierek—who waged an unyielding attack on the regime's inept economic policy—and the militant nationalist Partisans headed by the minister of the interior and head of the security police, General Mieczysław Moczar, a wartime colleague who had emerged as Gomułka's main rival after his return to power in 1956.[16]

In this turbulent decade, when domestic problems were escalating at an unprecedented rate, the balance of power within the PUWP shifted in favor of Moczar's Partisan faction. Hence, not only was Poland's Communist regime in desperate need of a scapegoat to assume the burden of the Party's errors and restore public support for the Party, but a troubled Gomułka, faced with internal rivalries that threatened to end his career and encourage Soviet intervention, also needed a policy that would win for him support from within the Communist Party, especially the increasingly influential Moczarite faction. In accordance with historic precedent set by previous unpopular regimes, blaming Jews for society's problems was the preferred solution to deflect responsibility.

Given the Jews' tragic history in twentieth-century Poland, along with their small domestic population by the mid-1960s—between twenty-five thousand and thirty thousand out of a general population of thirty-one million—it is difficult to understand why Polish Jews would be targeted by the Communist regime. Professor Zygmunt Bauman, who taught sociology at Warsaw University prior to his ouster from Poland in 1968, suggests that Polish Jews possessed particular attributes that made them ideal candidates for the scapegoat's role.

A scapegoat, asserts Bauman, must be sufficiently weak to allow aggressive actions to be safely unleashed against him; must be perceived as sufficiently strong so that victory over him can restore a feeling of self-esteem and supply a cause for pride; and must be accustomed to dealing with rhetoric used to describe the causes of frustration. In Bauman's view, Polish Jews met the requirements for each criterion.[17]

First, Poland's Jewish population, a small minority representing less than 0.1 percent of the general population, was "dispersed, integrated in Polish society and culture, united neither by a consciousness of national community nor by organizational ties." Second, despite not being numerically strong enough to resist state oppression, official Communist propaganda presented the Jews as a powerful group—militarily in the case of Israel defeating larger Arab armies, and covertly by alleging that Jews were capable of influencing world media and government policies. Lastly, Polish Jews were subtly accused of having promoted Soviet interests through the propaganda of such high-level conspirators as Moczar, who continually alluded to Jewish Communists who had returned to Poland from Russia after the war to do Stalin's bidding. In light of Bauman's criteria, Polish Jews were the perfect scapegoat in an atmosphere where anti-Semitism and anti-Sovietism flourished. This unfortunately also made the Jews an ideal political tool in the power struggle within Poland's Communist Party, the PUWP.

When the June 1967 Arab-Israeli War and official Soviet position against Israel and Zionists provided the perfect moment to implement such a policy, Moczar was finally able to carry out his long-planned anti-Jewish purge. Toward this aim, Gomułka's infamous "Zionist Fifth Column" speech of 19 June 1967 provided Moczar and his henchmen the thin veneer of legitimacy to go on the offensive against Poland's Jews. By unleashing a policy of anti-Semitism, therefore, Gomułka could satisfy Moczar's hunger for greater political influence for himself and his followers while encouraging their support and preventing political disunity from further weakening Gomułka's regime in the eyes of the Soviet authorities.

Anti-Semitism—A Potent Political Weapon

The existence of anti-Semitism in Poland can be traced to a number of influences, including, but not limited to, misguided Church teachings, fanatical nationalist sentiments, and jealousy of the perceived economic success of some Jews. But the strength of anti-Jewish sentiments among the peasantry was particularly strong. Europe had remained predominantly agricultural well into the late nineteenth century. Because the peasantry had not yet completely gotten rid of some of its more extreme religious traditions and superstitions, American historian Howard Sachar argues, "the medieval conception of the Jew as Christ-killer, as blood-sucker, as well-poisoner," had not completely disappeared. Sachar notes, "In the folklore of the countryside, the Jews continued to repre-

sent the incarnation of the devil." While this view may
have been declining in an increasingly secular world, it
still continued with sufficient strength, even in Western
and Central Europe, "to stigmatize the Jews as a people
apart, a people under a historic cloud of suspicion, barely
to be tolerated." These old suspicions occasionally flared
into "active hatred."[18]

Given the inherent dangers of such popular anti-
Semitic sentiments, therefore, political anti-Semitism
becomes even more sinister as the state's ability to exploit
popular anti-Jewish sentiments has the potential to incite
violence or, at the bare minimum, encourage an acceptance of widespread state-imposed oppression. While these
ideas were first introduced and discussed in chapter 2,
there is more to consider.

When it came to political anti-Semitism in Poland,
observes German historian Frank Golczewski, "It was not
the peasants who were interested in this problem, but
their political leaders, who could incite them to act vio-
lently." According to Golczewski, anti-Semites comprise
three distinct groups: activists, propagators, and politicians.[19] The first and most numerous Golczewski calls
violent "activists"—people incapable of independent
thought but who are easily influenced by anti-Semitic slogans and driven by an inner desire to act against people
deemed to be enemies. Such a person is the only active
agent because he converts anti-Jewish words into actions.
Those who encourage the activists are "propagators"—
people of influence in the community, such as teachers,
journalists, and the clergy, who hold positions of authority over the lower classes and, therefore, supply the
motives and provide the signal to act. But the most influential of all the groups is the third—the "politicians."
Though numerically the smallest, they do not have to be
persuaded of the correctness or validity of anti-Semitic

views, and they are fully aware that with the support of
anti-Semites they can accomplish their political goals.
Thus, "politicians," according to Golczewski's theory,
cooperate with Jews if it serves their objectives, but are
very quick to acknowledge the most radical views as soon
as they realize that this is the way to achieve political victory.

Golczewski's theory is compelling since it provides a
useful framework to account for the absurd policies adopted by Gomułka's Communist regime in the late 1960s, a
time when Gomułka was facing serious political trouble.
Nonetheless, what may have begun as a limited accommodation of Moczar's nefarious policies for Gomułka's personal political gain turned into a nightmarish scenario in
1968 for the victims, the nation's reputation, and Gomułka himself.

Immediately after Gomułka's speech of 19 June 1967,
Moczar's spokespersons, with the support of the security
police, proclaimed a violent "anti-Zionist" campaign of
slander and denunciation. Just as quickly they disseminat-
ed books replete with such absurd allegations that
Poland's Jews, having formerly collaborated with the
Nazis, were now working with the West Germans against
Polish independence.[20] This was only the beginning of a
reprehensible smear campaign that soon spread through
the media under Moczar's direction. The course of events
seems to corroborate Golczewski's observation that
"activists" require the stimulus of "propagators"—especially journalists—who are directed by "politicians" to
unleash their dangerous instinct of hatred. This frightful
scenario is made worse by a totalitarian environment that
provides tacit approval of extreme actions, thereby providing the regime—which controls domestic media and
police activities—even greater potential for state manipulation of the masses.

Government-sanctioned anti-Semitism quickly unfolded in three ways: Jews were dismissed from responsible positions in industry and government; Party insiders sympathetic to Israel were purged; and the activities of the Jewish Relief Organization were brought to a halt.[21] In 1968, once Moczar's Partisans learned that two Jewish students were among those arrested by the Mickiewicz monument following the ban on *Dziady*, the Partisans now had all the "proof" they needed to complete their goal. Hundreds, then thousands, were dismissed from the military, police, Communist Party, bureaucracy, academia, and the arts, just because of their Jewish origin, "political unreliability," or simply for defending their slandered colleagues. People who had for years done their jobs without fault were now attacked on the most absurd pretexts, and deprived of their positions and primary sources of income.

As news of Poland's campaign spread to the West, many universities, associations, and prominent people—such as Bertrand Russell and Cesare Luporini, member of the Italian Communist Party's Central Committee—voiced their outrage, without any effect on the intensity of the vicious campaign. As a direct result of the 1968 "purge from below," about nine thousand people—Jews and, in fewer numbers, non-Jews—lost their jobs.

While the anti-Semitic policy seemed to serve Gomułka's political interests by encouraging support from anti-Semitic elements within the Party ranks, it is useful to explore how his support base had become so powerful. After all, without Moczar and his strong following, it is unlikely that the relentless anti-Semitic campaign would have occurred. Therefore, in order to understand Moczar's central role in the strange events of 1967–68—which one journalist rightly described as "among the most curious in the history of Eastern European Communism"[22]—Moczar's gradual control of the Interior Ministry, its security forces, and the media must be considered along with the composition of his support base and its use of anti-Semitism as a weapon for achieving political power. These crucial issues are considered in the next chapter, which provides an important foundation for understanding how the situation in the Soviet Union—explored in detail in chapter 6—influenced the curious actions that occurred in Poland.

CHAPTER 5

Political Opportunism and Anti-Semitism
The Gomułka-Moczar Alliance

Traditional anti-Semites believe that if someone is Jewish, he must be bad, whereas Polish anti-Semites believe that if anything bad has happened, it must be the work of Jews.

— Alan M. Dershowitz, *The Vanishing American Jew*

Biographer Nicholas Bethell asserts that Władysław Gomułka's part in the anti-Jewish policy "was half-hearted and on the whole restraining."[1] While the extent of restraint exercised by Gomułka is subject to debate, what is perplexing is that Gomułka, by most accounts politically shrewd, would have ignored the inherent danger of Mieczysław Moczar, who as Gomułka's appointee in charge of the domestic security and police forces had direct access to the Kremlin. After all, Moczar's potential for disloyalty was well known. Moczar had been among the signers of the 1948 indictment of Gomułka for alleged "right-wing-nationalist deviation,"[2] which led to Gomułka's dismissal from his post as first secretary of the Polish Workers' Party—Poland's former Communist Party—and his subsequent imprisonment from 1951 to 1954.

As Poland's leader at the time the anti-Zionist campaign occurred, Gomułka must ultimately assume responsibility for what transpired. Determining how much personal responsibility he bears for policy formation is difficult to assess since Moczar—head of the nation's security apparatus with considerable influence over the media—had by 1967 effectively become the real power behind Gomułka's throne. Considering Gomułka's precarious political position in the 1960s, however, Gomułka clearly needed Moczar's influence and likely viewed him as a necessary evil. Given the reality of Poland's domestic politics, Moczar, having developed a strong following over a significant faction of the Communist Party and Polish society, could indeed help Gomułka maintain the status quo. It is clear that this quasi-alliance between two political adversaries served mutually exclusive interests—for Gomułka it was an attempt to maintain hold on power; for Moczar it was an attempt to seize it.

Moczar's Influence on Poland's Domestic Anti-Jewish Policy

Wartime leader of Communist military groups who fought the Germans on Polish soil, Mieczysław Moczar was born Mikołaj Demko, and took his new surname, "Moczar," from the *Moczary* ("Swamps") Communist partisan group he commanded during the war.[3] Moczar emerged by the early 1960s as head of the Communist Party's "Partisan" faction—comprised of former members of Communist guerilla units who formed the core of the security police after the war.[4] In this specific context, while the label "Partisan" was associated with Communist wartime fighters such as Gomułka, who took part in the resistance against the Nazis, the "new" Partisans surrounding Moczar in the 1960s were tyrants who were determined to rid Poland of what they perceived as dissent and subversion taking hold of the country.[5]

Augmented by young sympathizers, Moczar's Partisans were fiercely anti-reform, anti-intellectual, and anti-Semitic.[6] Their platform consisted of three planks: authoritarianism under Moczar's leadership, a discreet appeal to anti-Russian resentment, and unconcealed anti-Semitism.[7] Politically ambitious and hungry for personal power, Moczar had taken two important steps to broaden his appeal and cultivate a reliable organizational following. The first tactic was the alliance Moczar had formed with Bolesław Piasecki, an outspoken opponent of Gomułka who headed the nationalistic Polish Movement of Progressive Catholics—the so-called PAX organization. Established in September 1945 to promote cooperation between Catholics and Communists in the building of socialism in postwar Poland, PAX was from its very inception a manipulative organization with suspicious motives. Before the war, Piasecki had been the leader of a small, extremist Fascist youth organization, famous for its anti-democratic, anti-Communist, and anti-Semitic views, and largely modeled on the Italian Fascist Party. Despite the Holy See's refusal to recognize it as part of the Catholic Church, however, PAX held considerable influence.[8] With more than five thousand members, Piasecki's group desired a one-party system within a Catholic nation that stressed strong Polish nationalism and social equality, without the presence of Jews to distract from these goals. On fundamental issues Piasecki shared the same views as Moczar, as both believed in the historic concept of natural ethnic unity, an alliance with the Soviet Union for reasons of state, and in an authoritarian state as the protector of this unity.[9]

Moczar's second and perhaps most effective tactic toward achieving power occurred in 1964 when Moczar became head of the Union of Fighters for Freedom and Democracy—known by the Polish acronym ZBoWiD—a veterans' organization of more than 250 thousand members reflecting diverse prior political affiliations. Suspiciously, ZBoWiD's membership rose dramatically during Moczar's tenure, though it was doubtful that the ranks were being filled with former wartime fighters since no one could explain the criteria for accepting new members.[10] Even so, there were practical reasons for the appeal of Moczar's organization. First, ZBoWiD had considerable funds at its disposal, which were used to help needy members; second, it exercised patronage in allocating jobs, housing, and free private medical service; and third, it bestowed countless decorations for wartime services, which qualified recipients for higher retirement pensions.[11]

Moczar's Political Tactics and Cultivation of Power

Increasingly viewed as a symbol of national unity with branches located throughout the country, ZBoWiD had become a formidable pressure group and, therefore, a particularly important political lever in the struggle for power. Moczar used his position and strength of his organizational base as a launching pad for an assertive nationalism, which appealed to both Communist and non-Communist members among ZBoWiD and the Partisans.

As deputy minister of the interior from 1956 until 1964, then interior minister from 1964 until the end of 1968, Moczar had built up an almost supreme position of power for himself, an impressive network of informers, and a system of files on everybody who mattered in the country. According to Michael Chęciński, a former major in the Polish military counterintelligence service driven out of Poland as a result of the anti-Semitic campaign, Moczar's access to the personnel files of the security division gave him opportunities to exercise persuasion, gentle pressure, or even blackmail. Thus, not only was telephone tapping, police surveillance, and correspondence interception used to monitor new recruits, but the privileged security information was, in Chęciński's words, "freely used to discredit and immobilize opponents and to foster the promotion of the initiated into various key posts." As a result, nearly every party leader, Gomułka included, was encircled by intimates, even confidential secretaries, who owed allegiance not to their supposed superiors but to the police faction headed by Moczar.[12]

In view of the horrors faced by the Jews during the war, even more sinister was the Ministry of Internal Affairs' completion by the mid-1960s of a card index of Jews. With a staff of over two hundred, the "Jewish Section" of the Ministry's Department of Nationalities, headed by Colonel Tadeusz Walichnowski, compiled genealogical charts of the Jewish population aided by countless informers.[13] This index was an indispensable tool in the subsequent attack on Poland's Jews, since it not only identified assimilated Poles of Jewish origin, but also mixed marriages, converts, their children, and Poles with known Jewish relatives or "foreign" connections. Not unlike the Nazis, therefore, Moczar's security service was capable of supplying on demand a list of Jews employed in virtually any field, profession, or even Jewish students enrolled in university.[14] As a result of these efforts, during the height of the purge that swept the country in 1968, most public institutions received lists of Jewish employees based on the card index.[15] Not only could Walichnowski's department produce real—or forged, when necessary—"proof" of a Jewish grandparent, but also the addresses of Jews.[16]

In addition to trusted associates placed in key positions in the army and Foreign Service, Moczar had many Partisans in the mass media. Therefore, as the oppressive campaign became openly anti-Semitic following the March 1968 events, virtually the entire press joined in. The only significant exception was *Polityka*, a serious Party weekly whose editor-in-chief, Mieczysław Rakowski, a supporter of Gomułka, was incensed by Moczar's abuse of nationalist sentiments and anti-Semitism for his own personal agenda.[17] The relentless campaign soon grew out of control as Poles of Jewish descent throughout Polish society faced ever-increasing harassment and intimidation, made worse by government propaganda spread by journalists. Moczar's supporters in the press consistently denied charges of anti-Semitism, maintaining that the government was merely fighting Zionism, not the Jewish people. Yet while attacking Jewish nationalism the press published fierce attacks on "cosmopolitans," the Communist euphemism for Jews.[18]

The first post-World War II attack on the Jews began in the USSR in January 1949 when the Soviet press, led by *Pravda*, launched a campaign against "cosmopolitans" that was aimed initially at those in the artistic realm, a term of insult for those artists, writers, and critics who demonstrated an excessive awareness of Western art, writers, and criticism. The term's meaning was soon broadened, however, to include ideological and political "offenses," and then narrowed yet again to become synonymous for Jews.[19] With Moczar in charge, a similar use of the term found its way into Poland's domestic anti-Semitic campaign.

Under Moczar's control, the press naturally condemned the student protests, suggesting in various editorials that small groups of wealthy, politically ambitious students were to blame—a strategy undoubtedly employed to stress the differences between protesting students and the masses of workers whom the Party wished to win over—while playing down any fault of the government and the brutality committed by the Communist security forces. Likewise, articles in *Słowo Powszechne*, the daily paper published by the PAX movement, reasserted the government's anti-Zionist theme, that Polish Zionists aimed to turn intellectuals and youth against Poland.[20]

There is little doubt that Moczar was primarily responsible for the student unrest, since the militia's incursion onto the Warsaw University grounds turned relatively calm protests into street riots, and the brutal handling of protesters helped spread the conflict to other colleges in Warsaw and the provinces. Moreover, the initial propaganda directed against specific writers during the anti-Zionist campaign was started not by the Communist Party leadership directly, but by two non-Party papers, *Słowo Powszechne* and *Kurier Polski*, both under the influence of Moczar, while central Party organs took up the campaign a few days later. In the first phase of the anti-Jewish campaign, therefore, among the two thousand arrested students, some with Jewish names were picked out and "exposed" as the main agitators.

Though just one of numerous examples, an article in the March 11th edition of *Trybuna Ludu*, the Party daily, included a list of leading members among the student demonstrators, which seemed primarily intended to entice public opposition against Jews. The names of "notorious troublemakers" included Adam Michnik; Józef Dajczgewand, who had earlier organized a demonstration against Michnik's expulsion from the university; Aleksander Smolar, son of Grzegorz (Hersch) Smolar, editor-in-chief of *Folksshtimme*, a Yiddish newspaper; Wiktor Górecki, son of Jan Górecki, director general of the Ministry of Finance; Irena Lasota, identified as the daughter of a retired colonel; Henryk Szlajfer, described in the press as the son of a censor in the Main Press Control Office; Ewa Zarzycka, daughter of the prior chairman of the Warsaw

People's Council (mayor) who had been fired in December; and Katarzyna Werfel, daughter of Roman Werfel.[21]

The same article raised peculiar questions about whether or not the students' parents, who had occupied important positions, felt "guilty" for having educated their children in a manner that would lead them to express such hostility against society and the state. Such a tactic was certainly intended to cast public doubt on the high-profile Jewish parents' loyalty to the state, while also holding responsible many professors and university authorities—the intellectuals—for the youths' lack of proper education and their lack of discipline. For that reason, despite his tenure as former editor-in-chief of Party monthly *Nowe Drogi* and (briefly) *Trybuna Ludu*, and as director of the Institute of History of Polish-Soviet Relations at the Polish Academy of Sciences, Roman Werfel was expelled from the Party in 1968.[22]

Besides emphasizing Jewish names to encourage public opinion against the Jewish scapegoat, references to Michnik[23] and Dajczgewand neglected to note their working-class backgrounds. This tactic effectively ensured that focus remained on students, Jews, and the intellectual elite rather than cast aspersions on the workers and the regime. The government needed support—or at least indifference—from the workers to avoid total collapse of the political order. In fact, the primary reason the student demonstrations failed to inspire the nation to revolt was because the students did not raise their economic grievances as a primary reason for their demonstrations, such as housing shortages, meager scholarships, and a lack of jobs for graduates. As a consequence, their cries for freedom of expression could successfully rally the support of writers, artists, and scholars, but would fall on the deaf ears of a working class primarily concerned with the standard of living.[24] Only sympathy and moral support was engendered among the masses, therefore, not active protest in favor of greater political freedom and liberalization in cultural life. Since anti-Jewish propaganda seemed to successfully appease Moczar's followers, Gomułka's part in the anti-Jewish campaign must be carefully considered.

Gomułka's Role in Poland's Anti-Semitic Campaign

As leader of Poland's Communist Party, Gomułka possessed the authority to override any policy, no matter how evil. Since political actions tend to have complex motivations, it is possible that Gomułka, for whatever reason, may have lacked the ability to resist the policy of anti-Semitism that was being urged by Moczar. This is the view expressed by Nicholas Bethell, Gomułka's British biographer, who asserts, "Gomułka was no anti-Semite," but "was dragged along by events, by a situation he did not entirely control."[25] There is evidence to support this contention.

Prior to 1967–68, Gomułka's record had been exemplary compared to the Soviet Union's and many East European Communist parties. Not only was Zofia Gomułka, Władysław's wife, of Jewish descent, but Władysław Gomułka also had many close Jewish supporters and colleagues. When Soviet authorities suggested in 1956 that the Polish Communist Party put on trial two senior members of Poland's postwar government—Hilary Minc and Jakób Berman, both of Jewish origin—as scapegoats responsible for the miserable state of the Polish economy, Gomułka refused to do so.[26] Nonetheless, Gomułka did allow the 1967–68 anti-Semitic campaign to proceed. But did he try to stop it?

As the "purge from below" revealed the degree to which the Partisans had infiltrated the Party bureaucracy, Gomułka must have realized that the forces he had unleashed by his "Zionist Fifth Column" speech were now threatening his own position and the nation's reputation. That Gomułka's wife was Jewish unlikely contributed to a feeling of security. Yet Gomułka did make an attempt to dampen the hysteria. In a curious speech[27] delivered on 19 March 1968 in the Congress Auditorium of the Palace of Culture in Warsaw—before three thousand Party activists and a national television and radio audience—Gomułka defended his government's actions while he also attempted to reduce the anti-Jewish frenzy that he had helped unleash. Referring to *Dziady*, the student demonstrations, and the existence of "evil" Zionist forces, Gomułka's speech did not back down from the government's position, but rather reasserted the main aspects of the propaganda.[28]

Gomułka declared that students who were of "Jewish origin" and whose parents occupied responsible and "high posts" in the Polish state played an active part in the events of March 1968. On the basis of such allegations, Gomułka claimed that this was the reason why "the slogan of struggle against Zionism, a slogan that was sometimes misrepresented," had emerged. By blaming students of Jewish origin and their parents in this way, Gomułka appeared determined to justify the "anti-Zionist" campaign at all costs rather than publicly admit to having pursued a misguided and immoral policy.

Despite the Polish regime's anti-Semitic tactics, Gomułka tried to diffuse the anti-Jewish rhetoric. Strangely, he suggested that not one, but rather three types of individuals of "Jewish descent" or "nationality" existed in Poland, each deserving different treatment. By dividing the Jewish population into three groups, therefore, Gomułka could defend his government's actions while also attempting to reduce the fury of ongoing attacks on Poles of Jewish descent. The first category of Jews to which Gomułka referred was alleged Zionists allied with Israel. Gomułka reminded his audience that in 1967, which he described as "Israel's June aggression against the Arab states," there was a "certain number of Jews" who revealed in a variety of ways their desire to go to Israel to participate in the war against the Arabs. Gomułka went even further, however, advancing the charge that this category of Jews was "not linked with Poland emotionally or intellectually," but rather with the State of Israel. Gomułka declared, "They are surely Jewish nationalists. Can one blame them for it? Only in the way in which Communists blame all nationalists irrespective of their nationality." Gomułka then openly speculated that this category of Jewish citizens would leave Poland sooner or later.

The lack of subtlety in Gomułka's tone was unmistakable. The first "category" to which Gomułka referred was therefore clearly at risk. The only question left unanswered was whether they would be forced out or if they would leave "voluntarily." This would soon become clear. But the second category of Jews to which Gomułka made reference consisted of the so-called Cosmopolitans, who by implication could not be trusted because of the supposed division of their allegiance between Poland and Israel. Concerning this second group, Gomułka asserted that in Poland there was a certain number of citizens who felt like neither Poles nor Jews, a feeling for which they could not be blamed, declared Gomułka, since "nobody can make other people feel they belong to a nation if they do not feel this themselves. But because of their cosmopolitan feelings, such people should avoid fields of work in which national affirmation is essential." Gomułka's words indicated only superficial empathy for this supposed "category" of Jews, the so-called Cosmopolitans. By advising them to "avoid fields of work" and demanding undivided loyalty to Poland, the clear implication was that suspicion and oppression would continue.

Perhaps to compensate for this likely result, Gomułka made conciliatory remarks about the third category of Jews—the most numerous according to Gomułka—who had "sunk all their roots deep into the soil on which they were born and for whom Poland is their only motherland." Not only did Gomułka concede that many of these Jews held responsible positions in the Party and in managerial positions throughout the nation, but that many, "with their work and struggle," had also provided great service to the People's Republic of Poland "to the cause of the construction of socialism" in the Polish nation, for which "the Party highly [valued] them."

From his speech, it was clear that Gomułka relied on whatever rhetoric was at his disposal to deny that anti-Semitism was the government's official policy. After all, how could it be if one category of Polish Jews was being praised by the regime? While Gomułka's words seemed almost deferential on the surface, given the activities carried out by Moczar and the security forces, Gomułka's statements were empty of meaning and certainly lacked any assurance of safety for Poles of Jewish ancestry.

Undoubtedly aware of the domestic and international audience that would ultimately hear or read his words, Gomułka added remarks to clarify what he perceived to be the difference between anti-Zionism and anti-Semitism, likely intended to avert further attacks of anti-Semitism leveled against him and his regime. Despite what sentiments "Polish citizens of Jewish origin" might harbor, Gomułka stressed that the Polish Communist Party was "decidedly against all manifestations having features of anti-Semitism." Gomułka emphasized that the PUWP was "combating Zionism, as a political program, as Jewish nationalism," which was something much different from anti-Semitism. According to Gomułka, "It is anti-Semitism when somebody comes out against the Jews just because they are Jews. Zionism and anti-Semitism are two sides of the same nationalist medal." His words notwithstanding, Gomułka should have known more than anyone else that the official rhetoric had been emphatically anti-Semitic in tone and intent.

Since euphemisms for Jews were used extensively throughout the campaign, Gomułka's three-category "distinction" for Poles of Jewish origin is therefore not a viable defense. Thus, Gomułka's division of Poles of Jewish descent into three categories could only strengthen the attack on Jews rather than weaken Poland's anti-Jewish hysteria—assuming that was his true intention. In practice it had not always been so easy to determine to which "category" a person belonged beyond the fact that the individual was simply of "Jewish descent," as confirmed by lists provided by Moczar's Ministry of Internal Affairs. Furthermore, when Gomułka alluded to the category of Jews "who will sooner or later leave our country," the Partisan activists loudly demanded their immediate departure.[29] Hence, if Gomułka's speech of 19 March 1968 was intended to reduce anti-Jewish feelings among the Partisans, it was a dismal failure.

Whatever Gomułka may have truly thought about the merits of the anti-Zionist campaign, his statements concerning Jews and Zionists did not immediately dampen the anti-Jewish drive being meticulously carried out under Moczar's direction. Nor did his words stop Moczar's zealous followers' pursuit of power. As the purge spread through Party and state institutions in 1968, it increasingly became a witch-hunt fueled by animosity and personal envy. "Kangaroo courts," comprised of ambitious Partisans, sprung up in offices and government departments to determine who was fit to keep their jobs. Thus, the people declared unsuitable and sent away were not only Jews and moderates of all shades, but many people who fell into neither category, their only transgression being that they happened to stand in the way of a Partisan's promotion.[30]

Only when the political situation in Poland stabilized in the summer of 1968 did Gomułka appear capable of restraining Moczar's forces. As a result, the extensive anti-Semitic campaign that had consumed the mass media and widespread personal attacks subsided. Although anti-Semitic statements still appeared in the newspapers, they were less vicious, and while dismissals continued, their number was greatly diminished.[31]

⁓

While authorities within Moczar's Ministry of Internal Affairs carried out the violent clampdown of March 1968, these actions would not have been possible without at least the implied support of those occupying the highest positions in the Party. Likewise, if such policies had not met with Soviet approval, it is doubtful that they could have been pursued for fear of Soviet reprisals. If the Soviet Union had objected, Moscow could have demanded that the Polish regime cease its actions. In this respect, alongside Gomułka, Moczar, and other officials both high and low who carried out the Polish government's nefarious policies, the Soviet leadership must share responsibility for what transpired in Poland. As far as policies and methods of oppression are concerned, Soviet influence cannot be denied. The Soviet Union provided ample models for Poland's hardliners to follow.

CHAPTER 6

The "Zionist" Scapegoats
Soviet Political Anti-Semitism and Poland's Anti-Jewish Campaign

There may be some differences in what aspects of Jewish life anti-Zionists and antisemites hate. But these differences are of interest only to historians. For Jews the consequences are identical.

– Dennis Prager and Joseph Telushkin,
Why The Jews?

Zionists, Zionist Sympathizers, and *Cosmopolitans*—some of the notable euphemisms for Jews heard in countless Partisan speeches and government-controlled media reports during Poland's anti-Zionist campaign. Not only did they mimic the Soviet Union's official verbiage following the Six-Day War, but they also recalled Stalin's notorious post-Second World War attack on Soviet Jews for their alleged "cosmopolitanism," or acceptance of Western ideas. Just like Poland two decades later, Stalin and his regime used such epithets as code words to unite the masses against Jews—and "foreigners" in general—in order to encourage Russian nationalism. In the Soviet Union, however, a "Zionist" meant no one other than a Jew.[1] While Soviet anti-Zionist and anti-Jewish rhetoric was imitated by the Polish regime, Soviet procedure had considerable influence on Poland's anti-Jewish campaign.

The Polish government's strategy of oppression—including arrests on trumped-up charges, intimidation by the secret police, and public and closed-door trials—is reminiscent of Stalin's purges. Moreover, the effective eviction of Poland's Jews recalls Stalin's plans to banish Soviet Jews to remote parts of the Soviet Union. Such similarities are not surprising since the Soviet Union had played an active role in shaping Poland's postwar anti-Jewish policy. In July 1966 Poland's politburo, acting on advice from the Soviet Union, authorized a plan for a wholesale purge of Jews from official positions, which secretly led to the immediate dismissal of Jews from the ranks of Poland's security service.[2] Hence, Poland's 1967–68 overt anti-Semitic campaign, whether directly endorsed by Soviet authorities or simply influenced by Soviet historic precedent or policy recommendations, featured rhetoric and methods reminiscent of Soviet tactics.

In order to identify Soviet influences on Poland's conduct, this chapter examines domestic Soviet anti-Jewish repression from Stalin through Khrushchev, outlining Stalin's devious strategy to exploit Jews as part of his conquest of Eastern Europe. It considers the influence on the composition of Poland's leadership after the complex battle between Polish Communists who spent the war years in Soviet territories—"Muscovites"—and those who spent those years fighting Nazis within Polish territory—"Partisans." Also explored is the role of Poland's Catholic Church as the primary "opposition party" in Polish society during Poland's Communist rule for the complex accommodations government leaders made, with varying degrees of success, to convince the devoted Catholic population to support the Communist leadership. With this foundation, chapter 7 more closely examines Poland's repressive tactics in light of Soviet models of banishment and oppression.

Stalin's Anti-Semitism and Anti-Zionism

While the 1917 Russian Revolution abolished anti-Jewish laws, granted the Jews full civil and national rights, and even declared anti-Semitism a crime, in practice the courts were quite tolerant of anti-Semitic manifestations, and severe sentences in such cases were the exception rather than the rule.[3] Though Vladimir Lenin believed that anti-Semitism contravened the fundamental socialist tenet of equality, he also maintained that rapid assimilation of the Jews would strengthen the revolutionary cause. In order to expedite Jewish assimilation in the Soviet Union, therefore, sources that fostered Jewish identity—such as Zionism, Jewish education, and religious practices—were outlawed, and thousands of prominent Jewish leaders were arrested.[4] Although such drastic measures had a significant negative effect on Jewish life in the Soviet Union, anti-Jewish policies continued during Stalin's rule, often as part of overt campaigns of terror that contributed to Stalin's well-earned notorious reputation.

Like Poland in the late 1960s, Stalin needed an internal enemy—a "Fifth Column"—that could be blamed for problems in the USSR. This term originally applied to rebel sympathizers during the Spanish Civil War, when General Mola claimed that General Franco's supporters were advancing on Madrid with four columns, and that they already had a "fifth column" in the city. However, the expression had since taken on a broader scope to identify any group within a country accused of secretly aiding an enemy attacking from the outside. As already discussed, Gomułka repeatedly used this label during the 1967–68 anti-Zionist campaign in Poland, intentionally putting Poland's Jews in a most precarious position. To suggest that Poles of Jewish ancestry were "secret sympathizers" or "supporters" of an outside force capable of engaging in espionage or sabotage within Poland's national borders was a libel that could only result in severe consequences for Poland's Jewish minority. Such consequences had already occurred in the USSR.

Despite Lenin's denunciation of anti-Semitism as a ploy invented by the capitalists to distract workers and peasants from the class struggle, Jews had become convenient scapegoats for an assortment of failures of the Soviet regime by the end of the Second World War. Since many Jews had relatives or acquaintances in the United States and Israel from prior waves of emigration, Soviet Jews, numerically weak, could easily be accused of being "agents" of American imperialism or Zionist forces. Hence, Stalin's 1948–53 crusade against "cosmopolitanism" emerged as the first expression of an official anti-Semitic policy in the Soviet era.[5]

According to Stalin biographer Alex de Jonge, "anti-Semitism is a theme that runs right through Stalin's life." Stalin had never made a secret of his personal anti-Semitism. While still a young member of the Bolshevik party, Stalin often spoke critically of the dominance of Jews among the rival Mensheviks, echoing a popular saying that the "Mensheviks were the Jewish party while the Bolsheviks were 'true Russians.'" After the Second World War, Stalin's attacks on various minority groups were accompanied by a rise in his anti-Semitism, which "was popular and in keeping with the new xenophobia. This led to the murders of prominent Soviet Jews, arranged by Stalin, culminating in the notorious "Doctors' Plot" of 1952–53 that contributed to a wave of national anti-Jewish hysteria.[6]

During Stalin's vicious attack on "rootless cosmopolitans," Jewish intellectuals were arrested, exiled, and, in many cases, executed, while thousands of others were dismissed from positions of influence in government and the Communist Party. Not only had Stalin's animosity toward the Jews grown worse with age, historian Alfred Low observes, but it drew strength from "the Leninist conception that entire classes were guilty of a lack of loyalty and deserved severe punishment" to strengthen the revolutionary cause. Consistent with this thinking, therefore, Soviet anti-Jewish sentiments were deliberately heightened by the so-called Doctors' Plot of January 1953 when nine top Soviet physicians—six of them Jews—were accused of having planned to poison Soviet leaders in a vast conspiracy involving Jewish philanthropic and Zionist organizations, the Israeli government, and various Western intelligence agencies.[7]

Stalin's widely publicized allegations succeeded in bringing Jews under suspicion throughout Soviet society. Across the USSR, Jewish employees were ousted from various institutions, and many Jews were assaulted in the streets. Shortly after Stalin's death on 5 March 1953, however, *Pravda* and *Izvestia* published full retractions declaring the accusations against the Jewish doctors completely false and without any foundation.[8]

Stalin's libel, which served to isolate and vilify Jews as ready scapegoats for his unpopular regime, was carried on by Polish authorities in the form of an alleged "Zionist Fifth Column" that threatened Poland, laying the necessary foundation for the 1967–68 official anti-Semitic campaign. Within the Polish context, however, since strongly nationalistic Poles had resented Stalin's imposition of harsh Communist rule, Moczar and his followers sought popular support by linking Poles' hatred of Stalinism with the supposed "influence" of Jews. Nevertheless, without Stalin's prior devious plan to use the Jews as pawns in subduing Eastern Europe, Moczar could not have successfully relied on this tactic.

Stalin's Incitement of Anti-Semitism in Eastern Europe

Stalin's personal anti-Semitism did not prevent him from using the Jews to further his domestic and international goals. Considering the spread of Communist rule throughout Eastern Europe following the Second World War, Jews, because of their history of persecution, proved to be a useful tool and convenient scapegoat for Stalin's policies. "It was a brilliant move," suggests journalist Jonathan Kaufman, since the tragedy of the Holocaust ensured that Communists of Jewish extraction, regardless of how unimportant they considered their Jewish background, "would be fanatically 'anti-Fascist' and determined to root out any vestiges of the old systems." Moreover, Jewish Communists were effectively immunized from regional nationalism, which Stalin considered to be "the greatest threat to Communist domination," as nationalist feelings "always came wrapped in a parcel lined with anti-Semitism."[9] From Stalin's perspective, therefore, widespread Eastern European anti-Semitism would effectively prevent Jewish Communists from developing a following that could rival Stalin's influence in the Soviet Bloc.

Since the nineteenth century, Socialist movements throughout Europe had attracted Jews to their utopian vision of freedom from discrimination and prejudice. In the West, though the vast majority of Jews identified themselves as "middle-class liberals" and most of the Austrian and German Socialists were non-Jews, participation of Jews in the Social Democratic parties appeared disproportionate to their numbers. Howard Sachar notes, it was "their frequent intellectual superiority over their proletarian colleagues, the years of dedicated pioneering spadework they contributed to the socialist cause, that accounted for their remarkable influence, their authority, and their conspicuousness" in post-First World War Germany—and subsequently in France and Austria. Likewise, a small but significant number of Russian Jews during the late nineteenth century became attracted to Marxist ideas since the Jews of the Pale of Settlement had become among the most urbanized, yet poorest wage earners of any other ethnic group within the Russian Empire. Marxism had therefore become "the panacea for the nightmare of czarist oppression," suggests Sachar, and its plan for transforming society "appeared far more thoroughgoing than staid liberalism, and far more applicable than agrarian populism to the needs of the harassed Jewish working classes."[10]

In Poland and other Eastern European nations, therefore, left-wing parties offered Jews an opportunity for political liberation without anti-Semitic nationalism that tainted other political movements. Considering that centuries of anti-Semitism had contributed to widespread irrational hatred of the Jewish people, anxiety among Jews that oppression might continue after the Second World War was legitimate. This helps account for the attraction some Jews felt for extreme left-wing ideas.

Though the vast majority of Jews who survived the war in Eastern Europe justifiably chose to emigrate in fear of Communist rule and renewed violence, some chose to remain specifically because they believed in the professed Communist ideal of equality. Nonetheless, whether sympathetic or opposed to Communism, Jews who remained in Eastern Europe following the Second World War were united in their opposition to the Christian and nationalist parties that fought for power against the Communists. In view of Hitler's crimes, no Jew would be safe if there were a return to the type of nationalism that had taken hold of Germany and Eastern Europe in the 1930s.

❦

Despite significant positions held by Jews in various Communist regimes of Eastern Europe, most leading Communists—or Communists at any level—were *not* Jewish. Despite the relatively small number of Jews belonging to the Communist Party in Poland, Poles of Jewish descent were still widely perceived as outsiders acting as puppets for Soviet colonizers. Stalin's devious policies helped create this climate of suspicion.

It has been argued that Poland's 1946 pogrom at Kielce, in which dozens of Holocaust survivors were murdered, was prompted by Soviet agents in the desire that this would "ease" nationalist tensions and, as a side benefit, manufacture an excuse for continued Soviet military presence in Poland.[11] This violent anti-Jewish attack did appear to serve as an excuse for Soviet authorities to tighten their grip on the Polish security forces by suggesting that the Poles, even Communist Poles, were not capable of upholding law and order by themselves.[12] Furthermore, as Stalin's anti-Semitic attack on "rootless cosmopolitans" spread to Eastern Europe, not only were Jews dismissed from government and Communist Party positions in various Soviet satellite states, but similar objectives that led to Kielce may have been behind the staging of peculiar show trials of "Zionist conspirators."

While "Jewish Stalinists" had been considered trusted allies in the first stage of "sovietization" in Poland, Czechoslovakia, Hungary, Romania, East Germany, and Bulgaria, Stalin did not hesitate to sacrifice them. Encouraging popular anti-Semitism through the public punishment of high-profile Jewish leaders served to deflect Eastern European hatred of Soviet domination toward Jews. Perhaps the most notorious example of Stalin's tactic was the December 1952 trial and execution of Rudolf Slansky,

General Secretary of the Czechoslovak Communist Party. A Jew by descent, Slansky, together with twelve others—ten of them Jews—were charged as "spies, traitors, and embezzlers" and "Zionist agents" for supposedly plotting to assassinate President Klement Gottwald. All were hanged in Prague's Pankrac prison.[13]

Carrying out its anti-Jewish policy in 1967–68, Poland's leadership was undoubtedly aware of, if not directly influenced by, Stalin's anti-Jewish precedents of dismissals, arrests, trials, and exile. All were key elements in the Polish government's campaign. Besides Stalin, however, Khrushchev's policies also proved influential.

Khrushchev's Anti-Semitism and Anti-Zionism

Although Khrushchev's "de-Stalinization" campaign briefly reduced domestic anti-Jewish oppression, Khrushchev ultimately upheld many of Stalin's anti-Jewish restrictions in order to avert the political consequences associated with antagonizing pro-Stalinists in the Soviet Communist Party. Other considerations may have supported Khrushchev's reintroduction of state-initiated anti-Semitism as well, such as the serious economic problems plaguing the USSR that could no longer be blamed on wartime devastation.

Evidence for anti-Jewish scapegoating is incriminating. In 1961, the USSR introduced the death penalty for economic crimes like embezzlement and theft—an unprecedented act in peacetime when the nation's survival was not threatened. The crusade was notoriously anti-Semitic: Jews in Russia, who had traditionally occupied jobs in management and accounting, represented the overwhelming majority of those executed for economic crimes between 1961 and 1962, despite the Jewish population's miniscule presence among Soviet managers and accountants.[14]

This practice of pinning the cause of economic problems on Jews was emulated in Poland. As discussed earlier, Poland's economic difficulties contributed to the Communist regime's oppression of the intelligentsia and student demonstrators, while adding fuel to the anti-Jewish campaign. Blamed for Poland's economic crises, prominent economic reformers—denounced as "Zionist agents" and "revisionists"[15]—were among the high-profile victims of Poland's anti-Semitic policies. For example, Włodzimierz Brus, a leading Polish economic reformer who lost his university position in April 1968, was ultimately forced out of Poland in October 1968.

Though Khrushchev did not criticize Stalin's anti-Semitism in his denunciation of Stalin's "excesses" in February 1956, he also did not return to the kind of widespread terror and anti-Semitism of Stalin's era. Nonetheless, in the post-Stalin years of the 1950s, anti-Jewish discrimination in the USSR had resumed in administrative, government, and political areas. In a speech published in the Western (but not Soviet) press, Khrushchev defended this policy on the grounds that anti-Semitism would rise if Jews occupied too many important positions in Soviet society. Despite evidence to the contrary, Khrushchev publicly denied the existence of anti-Semitism in the USSR, describing such accusations as slanderous.[16] Here again, parallels with Poland prove unmistakable. Gomułka and Moczar, among others in Poland's Communist regime had advanced a similar defense as part of their propaganda efforts, despite the highly suspicious dismissal of thousands of Poles of Jewish ancestry from various positions in Polish society.

While his actions may not have been a result of anti-Semitic motives, as Stalin's seemed to be, Khrushchev, always the pragmatist, did advocate the elimination of Jews from important positions if it meant restoring the popularity of the Communist Party. For instance, given popular anti-Semitic sentiments in Poland, when Khrushchev came to Warsaw in March 1956 to attend Polish leader Bolesław Bierut's funeral, Khrushchev, citing the Soviet Communist Party leadership's more "acceptable" composition, expressed disapproval of the small percentage of Jewish senior officials in the PUWP.[17] Under Gomułka's leadership, therefore, the new Polish regime removed several leading Communist figures from the Muscovite group, some of them Jews, who had been associated with Stalin's implementation of Communist rule in Poland. But Soviet anti-Jewish policies, after being embraced by Moczar's Partisans, ultimately proved more destructive to the Jews of Poland.

The Partisan-Muscovite Rivalry

After the war, when Stalin was installing loyal Communist regimes throughout Eastern Europe, he preferred Communists who had been in the USSR during the war under his effective control over other Communist Partisan leaders—like Gomułka and Moczar—who had operated during the German occupation independent of Soviet direction. In Poland during the late 1940s, therefore, Stalin purged Communist Party members who had remained in Poland during the Nazi occupation—including Gomułka and other Partisans, who were imprisoned on suspicion of "nationalist deviation"—because they were perceived by Stalin as untrustworthy.

Having spent the war years in the USSR, the ruling Muscovites were more sophisticated in their outlook and less nationalistic than the Communist Partisans, and therefore assumed leadership positions in Poland as well as other Soviet satellites. Though most Muscovites were removed from leadership positions in Poland during the upheaval of October 1956 that brought Gomułka back to power, many Muscovites had actually worked for Gomułka's return. Yet neither the Muscovites nor the Partisans were uniform in their views on Stalinism, since each faction contained both hardliners and revisionists.[18] Only common wartime experiences distinguished the two groups. Nonetheless, like any good political manipulator, Moczar did not draw distinctions in his rhetoric against the Muscovites, particularly when he had a personal agenda to fulfill.

In 1967–68, to attract the support of the Polish masses, Moczar relied on Partisan journalists and spokesmen to incite anti-Semitism of a specific kind. Moczar sought to revive the old prejudice that associated Jews with Russian Communism and with disloyalty to the cause of Polish independence by hinting at a new "national" Communism cleansed of Soviet and Jewish "contamination." Toward this goal, Moczar's henchmen not only drew attention to the Jewish backgrounds of some reforming intellectuals, but they also focused on the composition and influential role of Jewish Muscovites, a group they blamed for imposing on Poland the unpopular brand of Soviet-style Communism.[19]

Moczar personally contributed to this effort. During a rare Polish television appearance on 5 April 1968, he suggested that those ultimately responsible for Poland's current troubles were "politicians" who came to Poland in 1944 with the victorious Soviet armies. Moczar declared:

> The arrival in our country, together with the heroic soldiers, of certain politicians dressed in officers' uniforms, who later were of the opinion that for this reason it was only they—the Zambrowskis,

the Radkiewiczes, the Bermans—[who] had the right to leadership, had a monopoly on deciding what was right for the Polish nation. This fact was, at that time, an expression of a lack of [Russian] confidence in us, and from that fact began the evil which lasted until 1956.[20]

Among the nine people Moczar mentioned by name, eight were of Jewish descent while the ninth, a non-Jew, had a Jewish wife. By linking supposed Zionists to the despised Stalinist regime, Moczar attempted to shift blame onto them for Poland's postwar position as a Soviet colony. Therefore, by attacking selected Jewish Muscovites by name, Moczar appeared determined to perpetuate his belief that had the power in 1948 been left in the hands of "native," or at least "ethnically Polish" Communists, the extremes of Stalinism might have been avoided.[21] If Moczar's activities as a senior "native" official of the despised security service were typical of "native" rule, such an idea is virtually inconceivable.

Whereas the first three "Muscovite" presidents of Communist Poland—Bolesław Bierut (1944–1952), Aleksander Zawadzki (1952–1964), and Edward Ochab (1964–1968)—were not of Jewish descent, Poles of Jewish origin, such as Jakób Berman, Hilary Minc, Roman Werfel, and Roman Zambrowski, were represented in the political hierarchy of the People's Republic of Poland.[22] Since some influential Muscovites were indeed of Jewish origin, Moczar used this fact to argue for the elimination from Poland of all Jews together with the old leadership.

Moczar's plan gained Gomułka's favor for pragmatic political reasons. During the anti-Jewish campaign, Gomułka sought support among the Partisan faction since the majority of the Jewish party activists, regardless of their political pasts, had become the center of the "liberal" opposition to Gomułka after 1958–59. By the 1960s, therefore, Gomułka, feeling increasingly threatened by the "revisionists," achieved a temporary tactical alliance with Moczar, but without directly approving of his anti-Semitism.[23]

❧

Although Stalin's persecution of Jews reflected his personal anti-Semitic bias, his actions also underscored his fear that Jewish nationalist sentiments—rejuvenated by the emergence of Israel—would inspire the same reaction among other national minorities, representing a potential threat to the absolute power of the Communist Party. In the case of Poland, however, such a fear was unjustified since neither ethnic minorities nor the emergence of Israel as a powerful entity in the Near East were obvious threats to Poland's regime. As mentioned previously, the leadership of the Polish Communist Party feared instability caused by rising discontent among intellectuals, workers, and the younger generation. Yet they had already become justifiably impatient with the policies of the existing Communist regime. Moreover, the danger of growing unrest caused Gomułka to worry about the rising threat of powerful factions inside the Communist Party as well as the continued strength of Poland's influential Catholic Church.

While the Church of Rome's involvement in Polish affairs goes back to the year 966—when Poland's first ruler, Prince Mieszko I, converted to Christianity—the relationship between Poland and Catholicism gained considerable strength between 1795 and 1918, during the period of Poland's partition among the German, Russian, and Austrian empires. Like the Catholic Church in Ireland, notes British journalist Christopher Cviic, "the Polish Church came to be regarded by the people as the chief guardian of the nation's culture and language and thus, also, of its identity."[24] Given its unrivaled influence over the hearts and minds of a large segment of the Polish population, therefore, the Church emerged as a powerful challenge to the Communist authorities.

The Polish Catholic Church: Communism's Popular Opposition

The Roman Catholic Church in Poland, historically the strongest Church in Eastern Europe, had been substantially strengthened as a result of postwar border changes that concentrated within the new Polish frontier a very large percentage of a population that embraced the Catholic faith. Indeed, the Roman Catholic Church's position in Poland was stronger after the Second World War than at any prior period in the Polish Church's thousand-year history, primarily because of the ethnic and cultural transformation that occurred due to the effects of the war, followed by a significant westward border shift and substantial emigration and internal migration.

Polish Catholics formed barely 50 percent of the population in 1773 at the time of Poland's First Partition, and by 1921 they formed just 66 percent. But by 1946, as a consequence of the Nazi regime's annihilation of Poland's Jews—who had comprised 10 percent of Poland's population just prior to the war—and the expulsion of the Ukrainians and Germans from the new borders, Polish Catholics formed nearly 96 percent of the population. For the first time in history, Poland was an undisputed "Catholic" country.[25]

Even with the imposition of Communist rule in the late 1940s, the majority of Poles looked to the Church not only for spiritual guidance, but also for political direction. Concerned about the Church's broad popular support in

Poland, the Communist regime, desiring unrivaled authority, tried to weaken the Church from within. Party leaders attempted this by making use of Bolesław Piasecki's PAX organization, which had been established in September 1945 to encourage cooperation between Catholics and Communists in building socialism in Poland. The ultimate goal was the effective neutralization of the Catholic Church's power in Poland.[26]

While the Polish Church lacked paper and printing facilities, PAX, supported by government financing, had become a thriving publishing house distributing what appeared to be Catholic Christian theology. The materials contained a strong underlying theme termed by PAX as "state instinct," which prohibited any challenge to the Party or the government as a danger to the state itself.[27] But the various attempts to repress the Church proved unsuccessful. After Gomułka came to power in 1956 and freed from internal exile Cardinal Stefan Wyszyński, archbishop of Warsaw and Gniezno and primate of Poland, a 1950 agreement accommodating Church activities was renewed, with the added provision that granted the state veto power over Church appointments. In 1956 Gomułka was happy to have the Polish Church's endorsement, which he needed to strengthen his rule.

The relaxed relations between church and state did not last very long following the Church's successful challenge to the regime's authority. Since at least 1961, Poland's official state atheism fought against the Catholic hierarchy for control over the souls of the entire nation. Yet the resulting elimination of religious instruction in schools led to the building of a network of so-called catechism points for after-school religious instruction at churches, which again served to strengthen the link between church and country. Rather than reduce the influence of the Roman Catholic Church, therefore, the government's abolition of religious instruction actually contributed to the increase of religious influence: the government's actions not only increased the determination of Catholics to defend their educational role, but also further stimulated the process of the Church's development into an autonomous organization within society.[28] The Church had indeed emerged as Poland's true opposition party.

Given the population's increasing discontent with the Communist regime's political, social, and economic policies, combined with its support of the Catholic Church, tensions in church-state relations continued to rise throughout the 1960s. Harassment of the Church resumed in 1966, after Cardinal Wyszyński and thirty-five Polish bishops wrote an "open letter" in November 1965 to all German bishops proposing mutual reconciliation and mutual forgiveness of past sins each nation had inflicted on the other. By taking this action, Poland's bishops had effectively provided the government with ammunition to use against the Church.

Gomułka, angered by the Church's encroachment on the state's authority, launched a swift propaganda campaign against the Polish bishops. He accused them of treasonous behavior, denied Cardinal Wyszyński a passport to travel to Rome, and refused an invitation to Pope Paul VI, who had intended to come to Poland for the 1966 celebrations marking the millennium of Poland's conversion to Christianity. Gomułka's campaign misfired, however, for as soon as the Party attacked the Episcopate, or the collective body of bishops, Catholic opinion quickly and fiercely swung back to the side of the Church, which had briefly waned because of immense hatred of Germans for wartime atrocities committed in Poland. Hence, the main celebrations of the millennium held on 26 August 1966 at Poland's national Catholic shrine at Jasna Góra in Często-chowa, near Cracow, became an impressive expression of popular backing for the Church, with more than a million people from all over Poland arriving to attend the ceremonies.[29]

As an organization virtually free of government control, the Church absorbed public dissatisfactions with the regime's policies and became an outlet for them, which enhanced the Church's authority in Communist Poland. By the late 1960s, therefore, the Church indirectly benefited from both the PUWP's internal conflict waged between Gomułka and Moczar's Partisans, and the regime's subsequent preoccupation with "revisionism" and the "Zionist threat," since these distractions prevented the government from concentrating on its struggle with the Church. In the 1960s, however, the Catholic Church in Poland had also supported the intelligentsia's demands for freedom of conscience.

Responding to the government's vicious crackdown of the student protests of March 1968, Cardinal Wyszyński and Cardinal Karol Wojtyła, archbishop of Cracow (who in 1978 was elected Pope John Paul II) wrote a letter on behalf of the Church to Prime Minister Józef Cyrankiewicz on 21 March 1968 condemning the regime's tactics, demanding the release of arrested students, and appealing for more truthful reporting in the press.[30] While the letter was ignored, on the subject of the anti-Semitic campaign the Polish Catholic Church's official response was subdued. But to its credit, the Church did declare support of Israel's independence when the domestic anti-Zionist campaign erupted following the Six-Day War.

Not until 1968, when the Jews were being swiftly forced out of Poland, did the Church finally speak out against the government's reprehensible anti-Semitic course of action.[31] Yet publications close to the Church, such as *Tygodnik Powszechny* and *Więź*, had allowed opposition intellectuals—several of Jewish ancestry, such as Adam Michnik—to write under pseudonyms, since they had been forbidden to contribute to Party-controlled periodicals.

By the late 1960s, therefore, in order to maintain control over Poland, Gomułka had to contend with a public increasingly opposed to Communist rule, dissent from within the Communist Party, the concerns of the Kremlin, and Poland's powerful Church. Despite Gomułka's political success in retaining control over the Party, the 1967–68 anti-Semitic campaign did not deflect attention from Gomułka's—and Poland's—mounting troubles. Instead, Moczar's effective expulsion of Poland's Jews only served to further tarnish Poland's and Gomułka's international reputations.

CHAPTER 7

Exile of Jews
A Bureaucratic Solution
for Irrational Hatred

*No one doubts—not even their enemies—that the Jews have been
the most creative of all the small peoples in human history. From
the prophets of the Bible to the rabbis of the Talmud to the poets
and philosophers of the Middle Ages to the writers, musicians, and
scholars of modern times, the Jews have always been startlingly
important in the spiritual history of humankind. Why this is so
remains a mystery. Some have found the answer in the destiny that
God ordained for the Jews. Others have found it in the persistent
pressure to which Jews have been subjected, almost always, by anti-
Semites. We find it in the continuity of the character of the Jews.*

– Arthur Hertzberg and Aron Hirt-Manheimer,
Jews: The Essence and Character of a People

Over the course of European history, many societies had
endeavored to remove the Jews from their lands for religious, economic, political, or outright anti-Semitic reasons. In 1290 the Jews were banished from England; in
1306 they were expelled from France; in 1492 they were
evicted from Spain; and in 1497, from Portugal. In fact,
between the forced exile from England in 1290 and the
1541 banishment of the Jews from the kingdom of Naples,
Jews had been forced out of most European lands from
England, France, Spain, Sicily, and Portugal, to numerous
German cities and principalities.

Though the Jews were ultimately permitted to return—in some cases after a few years, in other cases after a century or more—this pattern of evictions served as mere background for the immense tragedy the twentieth century would inflict on the Jews—the Holocaust. While the Nazis chose confinement and murder as the preferred means to rid society of Jews, other regimes like the Soviet Union and Poland relied on the historic precedent of exile. The habit of Jewish expulsion had indeed become an obscene and routine occurrence in history.

❧

Considering the pattern of anti-Jewish rhetoric and action that had taken place in the USSR, Poland was not particularly unique. A similar strategy of euphemisms, arrests, dismissals, and exile was used during Poland's "anti-Zionist" campaign. In Poland's program against the Jewish population, therefore, those responsible for its implementation did not have to look far beyond the Soviet example. By deliberately using terms such as "Cosmopolitan" and "Zionist Sympathizer," Soviet authorities could attack Jews—or virtually anyone deemed an opponent of the existing regime—without contravening Communism's ideological precepts against persecution on ethnic grounds. Given years of Soviet propaganda directed at smearing Jews under the transparent guise of anti-Zionism, Poland's 1967–68 anti-Semitic campaign was perhaps inevitable, particularly when combined with influential Polish anti-Semites blaming Jews for the implausible feat of having brought Communism to Poland.[1]

Following the Second World War, Joseph Stalin, determined that no unfriendly nations would rest along the Soviet frontier, strove to make the nations of Eastern Europe reliable Communist states under Moscow's direct

Palace of Culture and Science (*Pałac Kultury i Nauki*)

A huge concrete neo-Gothic building in Warsaw, the structure was a controversial gift from Joseph Stalin to the Polish people in the early 1950s. The Palace of Culture and Science served as a visual reminder in the heart of the Polish capital of Poland's position as a satellite state of the USSR. It currently serves as an office tower, museum, theater, and cinema complex.

control. While the transformation of Poland into a satellite of the USSR had been a fundamental objective of Russian policy since the days of Peter the Great, for Stalin, the conquest of Poland was crucial for the eventual control of all of East Central Europe.[2]

When the Red Army liberated Poland from the Nazis, it subsequently installed a Polish Communist government that upheld Soviet dictates—an administration comprised of a new set of ruling Polish politicians trained in the USSR whose loyalty was to the Soviet view of the postwar order. The stage was set for the implementation of official anti-Semitism in all of Soviet-dominated Eastern Europe. This was especially true for Poland where Soviet control was strongest, despite the fact that half of the six million Poles murdered during years of Nazi occupation were Polish Jews.[3] Anti-Semitism would henceforth be systematically spread throughout Poland's Communist Party and government departments until erupting in 1967–68 into an all-consuming public policy that affected virtually all areas of Polish society.

❧

Since the majority of Poles had remained hostile to Communism—widely perceived as an unwanted Russian export—Stalin's use of the Jews to establish Soviet control over Eastern Europe contributed to the strengthening of long-held popular anti-Semitic sentiments in Poland.[4] Thus, Moczar's manipulation of such sentiments, and Gomułka's subsequent approval based on reasons of political expediency, could not have happened without the Soviet Union's example, support, and Stalin's notorious postwar anti-Jewish strategy for Eastern Europe.

Targeting Jews: Soviet Plans and Poland's Implementation

The Polish anti-Semitic propaganda that alleged the existence of "unpatriotic" pro-Israeli Poles of Jewish descent and intentionally denigrated their reputation—culminating in the "excuse" for massive oppression and forced emigration—was not a new phenomenon in the twentieth century. In the USSR, the vilification of Jews through uncovering of alleged evil "plots" against the Communist regime was clearly calculated to malign the reputation of Soviet Jews and to cast aspersions on their patriotism and their rightful place in Soviet society. Not only did Soviet groundwork contribute to the nefarious policies of Poland's desperate Communist regime, but the idea to force Jewish emigration is also paralleled by Stalin's intended exile of Soviet Jews to Siberia.[5]

Besides his penchant for secret trials, forced confessions, imprisonment, and executions of Soviet citizens regardless of ethnicity, Stalin's solution for the masses of Jews included another course of action. In 1934, Stalin's regime declared Birobidzhan—an agricultural settlement on the Amur River in a remote part of the Soviet Union bordering China—as an autonomous Jewish region. Intended to divert Jewish nationalist aspirations to the USSR's advantage, this scheme was also an attempt to make Jews a "territorially-rooted nationality," more easily controlled by Soviet authorities.[6]

Although Jewish settlers to the area had reached thirty thousand by the end of the Second World War, the plan failed since Stalin's anti-Jewish measures had, by 1948, destroyed all Jewish communal and cultural institutions in the USSR, directly affecting the Jewish autonomous region. Birobidzhan community leaders had been arrested, exiled, imprisoned, or executed on a variety of charges

during Stalin's purges. Hence, by 1971, according to former U.S. senator Claiborne Pell, Birobidzhan was "Jewish
in name only," since of the region's 163 thousand
inhabitants, fewer than fifteen thousand were Jews with
"virtually no living culture of a Jewish content."[7] While
Stalin's death saved Soviet Jews from the ultimate aim of
Stalin's campaign—their full-blown deportation to
remote sectors of the Soviet Union—in Poland's case the
expulsion virtually succeeded.

Deprived of any means of earning a livelihood as a
result of the regime's repressive tactics, the majority of
Poland's remaining Jews were compelled to emigrate.
Between 1968 and 1972 the total number of Poles of
Jewish origin who left Poland was close to twenty thousand.[8] The vast majority of Poland's Jews left after the
witch-hunt began in March 1968, after which the numbers rose each month, stimulated by student protests that
provided the regime all of the ammunition it needed to
carry out its plans. On 29 March 1968 thousands of students were expelled from universities in Warsaw and
Wrocław, among other cities. Unable to find jobs, and
their meager savings used up, most of the dismissed journalists, academics, civil servants, economists, physicians,
engineers, clerks, and tradespeople—and their children,
who were expelled from universities—faced certain
poverty and continued oppression in Poland.[9]

Though leaving Poland was relatively easy according
to the official rules, it was an intentionally humiliating
process. The Polish authorities permitted emigration provided that Polish citizenship was renounced and Israel
was the destination listed on the exit permit. Some
authorities maintained that without such restrictions,
practically all Poles would request to emigrate or travel
abroad, but the true reason was more sinister. By linking
together permission to leave with the renunciation of

Polish citizenship, the return back to Poland was effectively blocked, thereby preventing Jews from ever returning to the People's Republic of Poland. As legal "noncitizens," therefore, the emigrants' exit permits merely stated that they were not of Polish nationality. But the Polish authorities did not care whether emigrants actually went to Israel or managed to obtain a residence permit elsewhere. What really mattered was that the regime could produce incontrovertible proof that these people—according to an official statement issued by the Polish Government on 10 June 1969—did not feel a connection to the People's Republic of Poland but rather a connection to the State of Israel.

While such documentation protected the regime from being accused of forcing the Jews out of Poland—which it had, in fact, worked diligently to accomplish—the method also prevented non-Jewish Poles from applying to emigrate, which would have caused a stampede among the seemingly endless list of disaffected citizens who desired to leave the growing oppression of Communist Eastern Europe for a new life in the West.

Unable to obtain work in their native country because of official pressure, Jewish emigrants, besides losing Polish citizenship for the "privilege" of being allowed to emigrate, were forced to pay five thousand zlotys—or about two months' salary—for an exit visa. As if such extortion were not enough, the emigrants, at their own expense, had to ensure that their former apartments were put in order for future tenants, since apartments were considered state property. Adding further insult to injury, emigrants had to cover the costs for railway tickets, transportation fees, and luggage crates, and if their children had completed higher education, their parents were obliged to repay the government for the cost of their studies.[10] Of the twenty thousand Jews who left Poland between 1968 and 1972, the Hebrew Sheltering and Immigrant Aid Society (HIAS) helped more than ten thousand of them find new homes in Western Europe, Scandinavia, Australia, and North America, and helped four thousand settle in Israel.[11]

Victims of Poland's Anti-Semitic Campaign

While the protests of March 1968 had intensified the anti-Semitic campaign, which saw mass arrests of students, the purge of professors, and political attacks against so-called revisionists,[12] many noteworthy figures were expelled from the Communist Party, dismissed from their jobs, arrested, tried, forced into exile, or imprisoned on trumped up charges.

Between March and June 1968 about eight thousand Jews in government, Party, administrative, and cultural positions were fired. Professors, factory managers, doctors, scientists, statisticians, all were expelled from the Party, and thus by direct implication dismissed from their jobs.[13] The few Jews who had still held prominent political positions, such as Leon Kasman, editor of *Trybuna Ludu*, were removed. Even Hersch Smolar, editor of *Folksshtime*, the Yiddish newspaper, was dismissed, and Ida Kaminska, head of the State Yiddish Theater in Warsaw, was forced into exile. Among Poland's "high-profile" victims, however, academics were most at risk.

Charged as "Zionist seducers of youth," many professors were forced to flee Poland and seek refuge abroad.[14] For instance, prominent Warsaw University faculty members Leszek Kołakowski, Zygmunt Bauman, and Stefan Morawski left Poland after being summarily dismissed on 25 March 1968. While some non-Jews, such as Kołakowski, had come under attack by the regime, the great majority of the academic victims were Jews, such as Bauman,

Morawski, L. D. Blaszczyk, director of the Institute of History at the University of Łódź, Julius Katz-Suchy, professor of international relations at Warsaw University and former Polish ambassador to India, and Adam Schaff, director of the Institute of Philosophy in the Academy of Sciences. Of all the trials to take place during the Polish government's repressive campaign, however, the most notorious among Poland's academic targets was that of Professor Józef Parnas, a leading scholar, scientist, and former university president, famous inside and outside of Poland.

The Persecution of a Polish Professor

For a year after the demonstrations of March 1968, Poland's courts were kept busy handling cases that, in normal circumstances, should never have been prosecuted. The trials began in Wrocław, Cracow, and Łódź in September 1968 and ended in Warsaw during May 1969.[15] While the courts should have been the place to test the truth of often obviously absurd charges, to defend the rights of harassed citizens, and to restrain officials consumed by power, this was not the case. The courts merely reaffirmed the "correctness" and "effectiveness" of the measures introduced by the Communist Party and the state administration, and as a result, no other authority was left to defend the citizen. In this regard, Poland's anti-Jewish campaign is a blatant example of the dangers of totalitarianism.

As the anti-Jewish campaign gained momentum after the student protests of March 1968, two important aspects became clear. First, regardless of how patriotic a record of service to the country, no intellectual—especially with Jewish ancestry—was immune from the wrath of the Moczarite Partisans. Second, the tactics employed were alarmingly similar to those used in Stalin's Russia. On both counts, the case of Professor Józef Parnas, prominent microbiologist and decorated Polish war hero, is particularly revealing.

Promoted to the rank of major in Poland's *Armia Krajowa*, the underground Home Army during the Second World War, Józef Parnas was medical officer of the Rovno Brigade. In 1943, while tens of thousands of people had succumbed to typhus in the Volyn region, Dr. Parnas saved most of the sick partisans in his brigade by manufacturing his own drugs. Later Parnas was credited with helping organize underground sabotage groups against the Nazis, and establishing contacts with the Polish émigrés in the USSR who had formed the Union of Polish Patriots.[16] For his efforts during and after the war on behalf of the Polish cause, Parnas was awarded Poland's highest state and military honors, including the Order of Polonia Restituta, and the Polish Order of the Virtuti Militari (Cross for Military Courage), an award equivalent in stature to the U.S. Medal of Honor and the British Victoria Cross.

In the years following the war, Dr. Parnas had earned an enviable position as a leading Polish scientist of international repute. As head of the Microbiology Department of the Lublin Academy of Medicine, director of the State Institute of Rural Occupational Medicine and Rural Hygiene, and former rector of Marie Curie-Skłodowska University in Lublin, Parnas had become equally well known within Eastern and Western European scientific circles. For his scientific work, Parnas received numerous honors from inside and outside the Soviet Bloc, including the Charles Darwin Medal from the Soviet Academy of Sciences in Moscow, and honorary doctorates from universities in Czechoslovakia. Not only was he made a fellow of both the Royal College of Physicians in London and the Royal Society of Tropical Medicine, he was also a member of the American Society for Microbiology, among other learned societies throughout Europe, and North and South America.

Despite all of his accomplishments, Parnas's Jewish ancestry, high profile, and substantial international con-

Prof. Dr. Józef Parnas, Prorektor (Vice Chancellor), 1949
Marie Curie-Skłodowska University in Lublin

tacts (he had traveled widely as advisor to the Geneva-based World Health Organization and International Labor Organization, and had been a visiting professor in

Stockholm, Rome, and Jerusalem) made him a prime target for state oppression. Dr. Parnas quickly became a high-profile victim of Poland's anti-Semitic purge.

Ever since renouncing his PUWP membership in 1963, Parnas was continually harassed by Poland's Communist Party and secret police. Though he was ultimately punished for his "defection" by losing the directorship of the Institute of Rural Medicine that he had personally founded in 1950—the first institute of its kind in the world[17]—and by being denied a passport to attend scientific conferences abroad, Parnas was not deterred from voicing his views. Not only did Parnas publicly declare his support for Israel's right to fight for its survival during the Six-Day War but in March 1968 he openly defended the right of Poland's students to protest against the regime. On 4 April 1968 Parnas was dismissed from his chair of microbiology, and was subjected to a smear campaign in the government-controlled press. Prevented from continuing his work in Poland, Parnas applied for an exit visa to go to Israel—the only possibility of leaving the country. However, Parnas was subsequently arrested, "with a show of force," in the opinion of Michael Chęciński, former major in the Polish military counterintelligence service, "normally reserved for ringleaders of dangerous criminal gangs."[18]

But why would the regime have blocked his departure? The answer is likely a combination of politics and self-interest. However desirous Moczar and his Partisan colleagues were in encouraging as much Jewish emigration from Poland as possible, they were in all probability even more interested in retaining the most prominent Jews in the country. If such Jews had been permitted to emigrate, their international reputation and credibility might have caused damaging reactions abroad against the interests of Poland.[19] But what the leadership had failed to grasp was that damage to Poland's reputation had already occurred.

Tried by a military court on spying charges, Parnas was sentenced to five years' imprisonment, a most severe verdict nearly twice as long as the maximum sentence of any other accused intellectual. While very few cases resulted in a verdict of not guilty, the majority of students and intellectuals, prosecuted under various articles of the Small Penal Code (MKK) and the Code of Criminal Procedure (KPK), received sentences from six months to 3.5 years. The longest sentences had been reserved for the known "March" activists, such as Jacek Kuroń and Karol Modzelewski, each sentenced to 3.5 years, and Adam Michnik, sentenced to three years, during their Warsaw trial of 2 January 1969.[20]

Although Parnas had been found guilty of espionage, nobody was able to establish on what grounds or evidence the indictment had been based. Colonel Nazarewicz, the prosecutor, was more interested in determining Parnas's Jewish ancestry, observes Chęciński, "than in the contents of his 'slanderous' letters, which were supposed to 'prove' his guilt as a spy."[21] Among the most contemptible aspects of Parnas's secret trial, like the closed-door trials of many arrested students, was that the prosecution was carried out on racial grounds, firmly based on so-called guilt by origin. If the accused were a Jew or had Jewish ancestry, such a person was deemed guilty of having committed a hostile act against the interests of the People's Republic of Poland; therefore, if the prosecutor succeeded in establishing that the defendant was Jewish by family origin, this proof was sufficient to convict and sentence the individual to three and a half years' imprisonment.[22]

Even if the accused were not Jewish, security officials often tried to establish a Jewish identity.[23] Although not of Jewish descent, Jacek Kuroń, arrested in 1968 for his role as one of the leaders of the student protests, recalls that the officers who interrogated him tried their best to find a Jewish name among his ancestors. "When they failed to make a Jew out of me," concluded Kuroń, "they wanted at least to turn me into a Ukrainian, all in order to be able to denounce me as an alien."[24]

In a mockery of justice, the courts' decisions consistently ignored Article 69.1 of Poland's constitution, which held that citizens of the Polish People's Republic, irrespective of nationality, race, or religion, enjoy equal rights in all spheres of public, political, economic, social, and cultural life. Moreover, the constitutional provision also proclaimed that infringement of this principle by any direct or indirect granting of privileges or restriction of rights, on account of nationality, race, or religion, is punishable by law.[25]

Since Parnas's "guilt" had been predetermined by the very regime Parnas had publicly opposed, no decision other than a guilty verdict was expected. While Parnas had received considerable negative press coverage when he was arrested, the press did not even mention his trial when it took place in the spring of 1969. This was also true of the student trials. The government-controlled Polish press would not expose to the public such an ominous indictment of the courts' proceedings. After all, the Party leadership had already demeaned itself. To now start accusing someone publicly that the person's mother happened to be Jewish, which was the apparent reason for arrest, trial, and conviction, would have been even more embarrassing.[26]

Targeted, arrested, tried, and convicted on trumped up charges of spying for the West, Professor Parnas was not just a prominent scapegoat of Poland's Communist government, he was likely set up to serve as an example to others of similar stature who harbored thoughts against the regime. His conviction was also likely intended to pacify staunch Communists holding anti-Semitic sentiments who wanted to see high-profile Poles of Jewish descent punished for their supposed unpatriotic attitudes. In either case, the outcome was intended to reinforce the stability of the Communist regime.

Yet in October 1971, after Gomułka's fall from power, Parnas was quietly released and allowed to immigrate to Denmark, joining his wife and sons, who had sought refuge in Copenhagen after Parnas's arrest.[27] He reestablished his career as professor at the National Veterinary Serum Institute and became chief editor of the international journal, *Historia Medicinae Veterinariae.* Though Moczar was still at the height of his power at this time, it was likely assumed that the trumped-up charges had already served their purpose, suggests Chęciński, "and that continued imprisonment of a world-renowned scientist was liable to do the new leadership more harm than good."[28] Parnas's release after having served three years of a five-year sentence was therefore an implicit acknowledgement by the new Party leader, Edward Gierek, of Parnas's innocence. After all, in the Communist world, spies were not released before their term of imprisonment was over, but in the very best of circumstances, they were exchanged.

The treatment of Parnas by Poland's Communist regime recalls the injustices of Stalin's Russia. Before and after the Second World War, countless secret trials and several public show trials took place featuring high-level Soviet officials—many of them Jews—as unwilling actors in Stalin's contrived performance of "justice." Andrei Vyshinsky, Stalin's notorious chief prosecutor, invariably obtained verdicts for the execution of the accused or, less often, more "lenient" sentences of decades of imprisonment. Although Poland did not execute its victims

Dr. Józef Parnas, 1988
Copenhagen, Denmark

as in the USSR, the manufactured evidence and railroading of defendants were just as reprehensible as the Soviet precedents.

Following his release from prison and arrival to Denmark, Parnas, in a letter to *Na Antenie (On the Air)*, a publication of Radio Free Europe, reflected on his three years of imprisonment as an innocent victim of the Party's rage. Parnas described his incarceration in the infamous annex of Mokotov prison of the Ministry of Internal Affairs, where many other arrested students, lecturers, and professors were also held. He wrote, "It was indeed the intellectual elite. Discussions conducted in Polish and other languages were at a high level. There were Poles, Poles of Jewish Origin, and Jews. An atmosphere of brotherhood and solidarity reigned." While Parnas noted the severe treatment to which he had been subjected, he differentiated among personnel who were sympathetic and decent from those sadistic torturers, which even included physicians who, in Parnas's words, "were more dangerous than 'educators,' officers of the Ministry of Internal Affairs." In Parnas's view, Moczar had concluded that those like himself in Mokotov were faring too well; thus, while some post-March prisoners were sent to the prison in Strzelce Opolskie, Parnas, among several leading Warsaw student dissidents, were "deported to the repressive prison in Barczewo." He was placed in solitary confinement, and his neighbor in the next cell was none other than infamous Nazi war criminal Erich Koch.[29]

Not only was Parnas's imprisonment unjust—simply another crime perpetrated by Poland's existing Communist regime—but being placed in a cell next to Erich Koch, who had been imprisoned ever since his extradition to Poland in 1950 for wartime atrocities, was also a terribly insensitive irony given the tragedy of Parnas's personal family history and his wartime military service on behalf of the Polish cause.

Personally appointed by Hitler to rule over the Ukraine, Koch had chosen Rovno, the largest city in the Volhynia District, for his headquarters. It was in this very region that Parnas, as part of the underground Polish Army's Rovno Brigade, had fought the Nazis. In 1959, Koch had been convicted of complicity in the killing of more than three hundred thousand Polish citizens, two-thirds of them Jewish. As was no secret to the postwar Polish regime, Parnas's mother, brother, and sister, among many other family members, had perished in the Holocaust.

CHAPTER 8

Political Anti-Semitism in Communist Poland
A Concluding Assessment

The communist Nationalists, who originated with the wartime Partisan Faction of General Moczar, made their abortive bid for power in 1968. They have been responsible for repeated anti-Semitic campaigns within the Party—even when no significant number of Jews remained; and have now surfaced once again in the Patriotic Association Grunwald. Whilst sharing the Stalinists' dogmatic version of Marxism-Leninism, they tend to be covertly anti-Soviet, pressing above all for a Polish Party for Polish communists. Their support lies among the faceless lower ranks, whose virulent resentments they foster.

– Norman Davies, *Heart of Europe:*
A Short History of Poland

Countless personal tragedies accompanied the thousands of Poles of Jewish origin who were forced into exile as a result of Poland's anti-Semitic campaign. More broadly, the events of 1967–68 were also a tragedy for Poland itself, as the actions brought an end to the promised reforms of October 1956 articulated by Gomułka when he returned to the helm of the Communist Party after the death of Bolesław Bierut. As Polish journalist Konrad Syrop observes, "Gomułka's 'Polish road to socialism' turned out not to be a broad highway to a better future but a narrow, meandering lane with Russian signposts. In Czechoslovakia it was the Red Army and its allies who strangled 'socialism with a human face,' in Poland it was the Party itself."[1] Not only did the Polish example ultimately occupy a well-earned position on the growing list of failed Communist regimes, but it also shows that wherever revolutionary ruling "elites" have unsuccessfully implemented a Communist state, tragic repercussions followed. As has often been the case throughout European history, the Jews of Poland, as scapegoats of a failing regime, paid the highest price.

While Polish Jewry escaped a nationwide pogrom in the late 1960s, what they endured following the 1967 Arab-Israeli War and the 1968 "March Events" represents a black mark on postwar Eastern European history. Although Jews faced discrimination and oppression in other European countries after the Second World War, they did not experience the kind of overt anti-Semitism that Poland's Jews experienced. Within less than a year, the Polish regime went from practicing a "covert-anti-Jewish bias" to enacting a policy of official anti-Semitism after the Six-Day War to implementing a pervasive policy of "institutionalized racial discrimination" after March 1968.[2]

The government's actions shocked many observers in the West, many in Poland itself, and certainly not least, the victims themselves. The purges were a tragedy for the thousands of assimilated Polish Jews who were either forced or chose to go into exile because of the prevailing climate of oppression actively encouraged by the Polish regime. Indeed, the government's anti-Semitic campaign of 1967–68 was arguably the most disgraceful episode in postwar Polish history.

Why the 1967–68 Anti-Semitic Campaign Occurred

In the introduction, questions were posed regarding domestic and international influences on the planning and implementation of Poland's 1967–68 anti-Semitic campaign. Reflecting on the content of the chapters of this book, they can now be addressed.

Considering Poland's domestic context during the late 1960s, it is clear that political anti-Semitism served various strategic interests. The peculiar circumstances of Poland's Communist Party, popular opposition against the existing regime, and threats to Gomułka's continued leadership of the Party led Gomułka to grant Moczar's Partisan forces the implicit go-ahead to carry out its long-desired anti-Semitic campaign in the aftermath of the Six-Day War. Through this tactic Gomułka successfully garnered support of dissenting Party members, thus retaining his leadership position—at least for a while—over an increasingly divided Communist Party. This satisfied Soviet demands for a strong and reliable membership within the Soviet Bloc.

Concerning international or external influences, since the authority of Poland's Communist government largely depended on the Soviet Union's support, Poland's oppressive domestic policy toward the Jews could not have happened without Soviet approval or, at a minimum, its indifference. It is not surprising, therefore, that Poland's domestic policy toward the Jews seems to have emulated, in official rhetoric and actions, repressive aspects of Soviet policy, and that Poland's Middle Eastern policy—clearly articulated after Israel's decisive defeat of the Soviet-sponsored Arab nations during the Six-Day War—followed Soviet dictates.

As described, at least two underlying premises guided the regime's campaign against Poles of Jewish origin. The first is that popular anti-Semitism had deep roots in Poland. After the Second World War, a segment of Polish society continued to hold negative attitudes against Jews, which were expressed in various forms, from a passive dislike of "strangers" to aggressive racist anti-Semitism.[3] Given prevailing anti-Semitic attitudes, therefore, Poland's Communist leadership likely concluded that persecuting Poles of Jewish ancestry would be politically desirable, as such a policy would garner support for the Party from a populace not particularly enamored with the Soviet-sponsored Communist regime. This points to the second premise. Besides anti-Semitism, anti-Soviet sentiments were widely held in Polish society.

Since Poles had never entirely embraced the imposition of harsh Soviet Communism in Poland after the Second World War, their resentment of the USSR's influence over Poland's domestic affairs accounts for the broad popular support of Israel against the Soviet-sponsored Arab armies in 1967. Strategically, the Polish regime chose to attribute support for Israel to a domestic act of treason by "Zionist forces," or a dangerous unpatriotic "Fifth Column," thereby appeasing Soviet authorities and providing the excuse to vilify Poland's Jews. As part of this process Moczar, among others, hypocritically blamed Jewish Muscovites for having brought to Poland from the USSR the more repressive aspects of Communism. Persistent sentiments of anti-Semitism and anti-Sovietism among Poles, therefore, help explain why Poland's Jews were chosen as scapegoats by the Communist leadership in 1967–68. The Jews' small population in Poland, and their obvious inability to defend themselves against the regime's overwhelming forces, were significant contributing factors.

The Political Downfall of Gomułka and Moczar

Although Władysław Gomułka may not have been an anti-Semite, as Poland's effective ruler he must bear primary responsibility for the intentional mistreatment of Poles of Jewish descent. Gomułka's June 1967 declaration of the existence of an alleged "Zionist Conspiracy"—a so-called Fifth Column in Poland—gave Moczar and his vocal Partisan forces tacit approval to carry out an extensive anti-Semitic campaign, which led to a purge of the Communist Party, government bureaucracy, and university faculties throughout the nation. Not only did the anti-Semitic nature of the policy satisfy Moczar supporters who filled the resulting vacancies, but it also laid the groundwork for Moczar's future bid for control of the Party, if that was his desire.

Having seized the opportunity presented by Gomułka's public "anti-Zionist" statements in the immediate aftermath of the June 1967 Arab-Israeli War, Moczar and his Partisan supporters went on the offensive and took the anti-Jewish policy to its extreme conclusion. While Moczar's propaganda campaign against the alleged "Fifth Column" had only resulted in fewer than five hundred Jewish emigrants in 1967, the actions of 1968 saw the emigration of thousands. The student revolt of March 1968 following the January closing of Adam Mickiewicz's historic play, *Dziady*—canceled because of audience applause at every anti-Russian line—led to the rapid acceleration of Moczar's fierce domestic anti-Semitic campaign.

Rather than bargain with the non-violent student demonstrators, Moczar sent in forces to beat and arrest them, a provocation that made the spread of student unrest to other universities a foregone conclusion. "Zionist" and Jewish elements were blamed for instigating the

demonstrations in the ensuing reprehensible media barrage—directed by Moczar's Partisans—quickly leading
to a series of arrests, trials, and prison sentences of many
of the accused. Nonetheless, other than removing thousands of Polish Jews from their positions and depriving
them of their citizenship, Moczar's plans ultimately
proved futile, as the Soviet administration preferred the
more reliable leadership of Gomułka—and later Gierek—
to Moczar and his fierce nationalism.

Although workers may have been sympathetic to the
plight of students and intellectuals in March 1968, they
did not actively support them through strike action.
Unlike Czechoslovakia in 1968 or the USSR in 1988, in
Poland workers tended to be the effective leaders of the
reform movement, with intellectuals subsequently asked
to join. In fact, the success of the Polish workers' movement, supported by the Catholic Church and significant
numbers of peasant-farmers who owned and harvested
their own land, reveal the extent to which Stalinization
had failed in Poland. Due to the demographics of Polish
urbanization and industrialization, the origin of the typical Polish worker was that of a Catholic peasant-farmer,
not the ideal background to ensure strong support of
atheist Communist rule.[4]

Not only had the Communists proved unsuccessful in
breaking the influence of the Church in Polish society,
which was particularly strong in rural regions, but they
also never succeeded in collectivizing agriculture. Hence,
the public disorder that resulted from the workers' extensive strike action against the regime in 1956, 1970, 1980,
and 1988–89 led to changes in Poland's political leadership in each case. Lacking the active support of workers,
March 1968 witnessed many intellectuals and students
injured and arrested, thousands expelled, and significant
numbers driven into exile, without any effective change to

the existing regime. It is therefore not surprising that from the late 1960s onward the majority of East Central European intellectuals abandoned the term "Marxism" in favor of the concept of totalitarianism to describe Communism.[5]

Given their disillusionment following the events of March 1968 and the Warsaw Pact invasion of Czechoslovakia in late August, many Communist idealists gave up the notion that the Communist Party would ever voluntarily reform the repressive aspects of Communism. The notorious campaign of official anti-Semitism certainly did not enhance their optimism. Nonetheless, change would indeed occur, perhaps none more dramatic than the revolutionary events of 1989. After the USSR's internal reforms enabled dissent within its sphere of influence, oppressive Communist regimes fell across Eastern Europe. Shortly thereafter, Lech Wałęsa—electrician turned leader of the independent Solidarity trade union—became the president of Poland in the early 1990s.

෴

Despite the threat of Mieczysław Moczar's power base within the PUWP, the open defiance of intellectuals, the massive student unrest of March 1968, and the reprehensible domestic anti-Semitic campaign of 1967–68, Władysław Gomułka had triumphed at the Polish Communist Party's Fifth Congress in November 1968 when he was reelected first secretary of the Central Committee. Gomułka's loyal behavior during the Middle East crisis, his firm opposition to Dubček's liberalizations that flowed from the Prague Spring, and his ardent support of the August 1968 Soviet-led invasion of Czechoslovakia that reinstated repressive Communist rule not only earned him the Kremlin's gratitude, but also brought Soviet leader Leonid Brezhnev to Warsaw to personally endorse his reelection during the November Congress. For his reliability as a leader in the Soviet Bloc, Gomułka was awarded the Order of Lenin by the USSR Supreme Soviet on 6 February 1970.

However surprising Gomułka's victory may have been to the general public and members of the Communist Party—especially the ambitious and ruthless security minister Moczar, whose highly nationalistic Partisans the Soviets viewed with suspicion—Gomułka's success was short-lived. Until the end of 1970, Gomułka had survived challenges from every direction. While he suppressed the so-called revisionists, accommodated Edward Gierek's Technocrat faction, and outmaneuvered Moczar and his Partisans, none of his reforms improved the economy.

Discredited in the eyes of many inside and outside the Polish Communist Party, Gomułka belatedly adopted new economic policies. In 1970, confronted by the economy's dismal state, Gomułka introduced drastic increases in food prices and higher work quotas just two weeks before the Christmas holidays; however, workers' riots in the northern Polish cities of Gdańsk, Gdynia, and Szczecin immediately followed. As a result of the protests, in which over forty people were killed, twelve hundred were wounded, and three thousand were arrested,[6] political rival Edward Gierek came to power.

While the effective expulsion of Poland's Jewish population initially helped Gomułka retain power by accommodating the objectives of Moczar's Partisans, it ultimately hurt him. By 1970, after everything that occurred following the anti-Semitic campaign, there were no convenient scapegoats available, and no prospect in view that might divert the workers' anger away from the political leadership. In this respect, the anti-Jewish policy had been too "successful." Therefore, after becoming first secretary of the Polish United Workers' Party on 20 December

1970, Gierek purged the Party of those held responsible for the December riots. Gomułka was expelled from the Central Committee of the PUWP in 1971.

⋘⋙

Although Moczar was the second most prominent figure after Gomułka in the Polish government during the 1960s, he failed to achieve greater power as a result of Gomułka's downfall. In fact, his career as an influential Party member would soon end. Because of the severity of Moczar's repression of the food rioters and strikers in December 1970, Gierek ousted Moczar from the Secretariat of the Communist Party in June 1971, dropped him from the Politburo on 11 December 1971, and in May 1972 removed him from the chairmanship of ZBoWiD, the influential veterans' organization.[7]

Rather than purge all of Moczar's old associates, Gierek won over most of them with promotions to higher posts and various state honors. Regarding the threat of ZBoWiD, Gierek took away virtually all of its powers by setting up a new ministry, staffed with his own trusted members, to deal with former servicemen's welfare and distribute patronage.

Gierek also discontinued anti-Jewish propaganda in the press and other media. In December 1971, Edward Ochab—an influential former president of Poland's Council of State who had resigned from Gomułka's government on 8 April 1968—had circulated a letter among Party Congress members that accused Gomułka of having used anti-Zionism as a cover-up for anti-Semitism, drawing direct parallels between Gomułka's methods and Stalin's "Doctors' Plot." But such efforts came too late to help Poland's Jews.

Given the few Jews who had remained in Poland, it appeared that the millennial era of Jewish life in the Polish state was effectively over. This sad reality was hard to dispute since Jewish religious life had indeed disintegrated. By 1971, while continuing emigration reduced the membership of the few existing synagogues, no rabbis or cantors were left to conduct services in the very few still functioning. Even the Jewish retirement home in Warsaw, built by the American Jewish Joint Distribution Committee, was opened to non-Jews. Jewish culture in Poland was irreparably damaged. There were no Jewish schools, and most Jewish cultural programs—choirs, drama circles, and art ensembles—had been disbanded.

Though Gomułka's downfall in 1970 was largely due to his inability to effectively deal with domestic unrest, Edward Gierek would face a similar fate. In September 1980, when confronted with widespread worker demonstrations, Gierek lost his position as first secretary. With the rise to prominence of the Solidarity trade union and political faction in the early 1980s, a significant challenge to the repressive rule of Poland's Communist regime had taken firm hold of the nation. This movement, followed by the revolutionary demise of Communism throughout Eastern Europe in 1989, saw the long-awaited overthrow of Poland's Communist government.

The Launch of a New Era

After Poland's revolutionary transformation in 1989, such legendary dissidents as Jacek Kuroń and Adam Michnik, their reputations restored in post-Communist Poland, reemerged from obscurity to assume senior positions in the new political environment. Michnik, who spent many years in prison for his opposition to the repressive regime, was a member of the first non-Communist Parliament from 1989 to 1991. Today he serves as editor-in-chief of *Gazeta Wyborcza*, the first independent Polish newspaper and Solidarity's former official newspaper, now among Europe's highest circulating dailies. Anti-Communist dissident Jacek Kuroń became minister of labor in 1993 and, nominated by the main opposition party, was an unsuccessful candidate for president of Poland in 1995.

In this new political climate, even Professor Parnas— completely exonerated of all of the false charges stemming from the 1967–68 anti-Semitic campaign and publicly rehabilitated by Poland's Supreme Court after the fall of the Communist regime—returned to Poland for brief visits in the early 1990s to receive honors and deliver lectures.[8]

Thirty years after the 1968 "March Events," the post-Communist leadership recognized this shameful period in Poland's recent history. On 8 March 1998, commemorating the thirtieth anniversary of the day when protesting Warsaw students were first attacked by the Communist regime, President Aleksander Kwaśniewski—a former Communist turned Social Democrat—declared that Polish citizenship would be restored to victims forced out of Poland as a consequence of the anti-Jewish campaign. Not everyone supported Kwaśniewski's decision, however. Some commentators, mainly those on the right of the political spectrum, asserted that the events of 1968 were typical of the Communist system as a whole and that Communism, not Poland, must bear the blame.[9]

Though the population of Jews that remained in Poland was very small—the best estimate in 1971 was about eight thousand, a mere fraction of the 3.3 million before the Second World War—anti-Semitism did not disappear from the country. Anti-Zionist and anti-Semitic propaganda made a return appearance in the early 1980s, when the extremist anti-Solidarity Grunwald Patriotic Union, formed in 1981, distributed leaflets and posters throughout Warsaw denouncing the Jews for attempting to seize power through the Solidarity Trade Union. Recalling the rhetoric of 1968, "Zionist" was again used as a blatant code word for "Jew."[10] While the divided Party leadership had initially avoided taking sides for or against Grunwald, the Soviet press enthusiastically endorsed the "anti-Zionist" propaganda, which provided Polish hardliners the cue to echo anti-Semitic slogans. Similar to the tactics used in 1967–68, significant efforts were made by some factions to discredit Solidarity activists in the eyes of the population by charging that they were Jews or controlled by Zionists who wanted to destroy Poland.[11] Though some significant Solidarity activists like Adam Michnik and Bronisław Geremek were of Jewish descent, the vast majority, just as during the 1968 student protests, was not Jewish.

In response to this backward trend, there were some encouraging developments. Many Catholic intellectuals harshly condemned Polish anti-Semitism, and several senior members of Poland's Catholic clergy did the same. Cardinal Wyszyński, the Polish primate, delivered a sermon on 1 March 1981 in which he quoted Julian Tuwim, among Poland's greatest modern poets, who had often been a target of anti-Semitic attacks. Even Mieczysław Moczar conceded, in an unsuccessful bid to be reelected to the Party's Central Committee in July 1981, that it was no longer possible in the current climate to incite widespread anti-Semitic attitudes in Poland.[12] Indeed, for Poland as well as its minuscule population of Jews, these were positive trends.

Despite the epoch of revolutionary change that would soon occur, the specter of anti-Semitism did not disappear in the post-Communist era. Since the 1990s, though only a few thousand Jews continue to reside in Poland, an anti-

Semitic element is still present in the form of a variety of right-wing political parties. However, they appear to represent a small proportion of the Polish electorate.

CHAPTER 9

From Persecution to Acceptance
Polish Jewry and Cultural Renewal
in Post-Communist Poland

*The knowledge attained, and the attitudes expressed toward Jews
and Judaism by Poles, both in Poland and abroad, related in the
final analysis to the formulation of a reconceptualized Polish
national, religious, and ethnic identity. Consequently, coming to
grips with the historical experience and the spiritual heritage of
Polish Jewry is not a marginal affair for Poles; it is a vital issue
that strikes at the heart of Polish self-identity. Those who avoid it
risk impeding the emergence of a new Poland.*

– Byron L. Sherwin, *Sparks Amid the Ashes:
The Spiritual Legacy of Polish Jewry*

During my travels in Poland in the summer of 1988, it
was obvious to me that society was in turmoil. Stores
were empty, restaurants offered very little selection or
variety, and people appeared despondent. The atmosphere
was dark. In that fateful year, the last for Communism, I
saw firsthand Warsaw and Cracow's dilapidated condi-
tion. The unease in Poland was palpable. When revolutionary political events rapidly unfolded the following
year, I was not surprised. However, what did take me
aback was witnessing anti-Semitism in Poland with my
own eyes and ears.

As I stood in line at a Cracow taxi stand, a bus with Hasidic Jews from America pulled up and parked. When the bearded men dressed in traditional black coats got off the bus at the rest stop, a small group of Poles began trickling out of a nearby pub, yelling slurs at these tourists they had never met before. One lone voice among the drunken mob tried to quell their taunts with cries of, "Leave them alone; they're spending dollars in our country!" However, this solitary figure was drowned out by the intoxicated masses, whose competing shouts were considerably louder and vastly more intimidating. When these targeted tourists realized what was happening—or perhaps, more ominously, what *could* happen—they quickly boarded their bus and moved on. Following this surreal episode I wondered, if this group of religious American Jews had not decided to quickly pack up and leave, could a pogrom have occurred? Anything was possible since no police were nearby. Such an unpleasant incident only proves that the vestiges of anti-Semitism continue to exist for some Poles, even if alcohol was the necessary stimulus to unleash the venomous words expressed by this particular crowd.

What can Poland—and other nations where this scourge persists—do about quelling anti-Semitism? In a Europe undergoing rapid change, there are measures nations can take to help reduce the prevalence of anti-Semitism and other forms of ethnic hatred from spreading, or at least from poisoning the minds of younger generations. One antidote is education. People might be less likely to attack any perceived "other"—or supposed "foreign" group—if they understand and appreciate the valued contributions the long-beleaguered Jewish people have made to the country's historic development. Before exploring Poland's efforts toward this end, Poland's post-Communist sociopolitical transformation is described together with a reflection on the present state of Poland's Jewish community.

Standing in line for a taxi at Cracow's
Small Market Square (Mały Rynek)

❧

After the dramatic conclusion of oppressive Communist rule, the Third Republic of Poland—*Trzecia Rzeczpospolita*—emerged in 1989. Even today, well over a decade later, the country continues its efforts to shed the residue of decades of Communism. In the interim, however, who could have foreseen that Poland would not only be embraced as a loyal member of the NATO military alliance, but also be invited to membership in the European Union's economic bloc? While these developments are certainly encouraging, Poland must maintain strong democratic ideals where respect for human rights is not merely a lofty goal, but a permanent fact, in order to continue along the positive progressive course decisively marked by its formal inclusion in the European Union in 2004.

A pedestrian street in Warsaw

During a two-day referendum held on 7–8 June 2003, Poles gave a resounding vote of approval to Poland's membership in Europe's massive economic alliance, with 77 percent choosing yes. Given a 59 percent voter turnout, this result was among the strongest of the group of nations destined to join the EU on 1 May 2004. If the revolutionary events of 1989 were only an indication of the failure of Poland's Communist rule, official membership in the European Union serves as final confirmation, ending fifteen years of sporadic uncertainty.

If Poland wishes to take on a serious role in European and world affairs within the "New Europe" of the twenty-first century, it must face its past. The continuous presence and cultural influences of Polish Jews need to be acknowledged, tolerated, embraced, and respected by the masses so that anti-Semitism, along with other prejudice and active discrimination, no longer plays a part in official political rhetoric. In time, political rhetoric should also dampen popular expressions of these antiquated sentiments. Unprejudiced education may ultimately prove the only way to achieve permanent, long-term change. But how Poland reconciles its Jagiellonian and First Republican history of toleration and multiculturalism with its Communist era of repression, isolationism, and intolerance, is a fundamental concern that remains to be determined. Such a resolution will prove to be among the most important steps in helping Poland come to terms with its past, understand its present, and achieve a better future.

Polish-Jewish Life After Communism

The collapse of Communism ended decades of totalitarianism and launched a new Polish renaissance where intellectual and religious freedom once again became an accepted principle of the state. Throughout the nation Poles reacted differently to these changes, but many who had suffered from historic repression, such as Poles of Jewish ancestry, took the opportunity to reassert their identities and cultural values within a nation they still considered their home.

In the aftermath of Communism's demise, what is the status of Poland's Jews? The arrival to Warsaw of Rabbi Pinchas Menachem Joskowicz—a Holocaust survivor who had gone to Israel after his liberation from the Nazi death camp of Auschwitz—was of great symbolic significance. He became Poland's chief rabbi in the late 1980s and sought to help bring about a revival of Jewish identity and culture among the small group of Jews who had remained in Poland. Although he—together with the position of "Chief Rabbi of Poland"—has since retired, New York-born Rabbi Michael Schudrich presently serves Warsaw's Jewish community.

As of 1994 the number of Jews in Poland was a mere thirty-five hundred out of a general population of nearly forty million.[1] Considering that not every Jew registers with communities, and that many Poles of Jewish descent have not publicized their family origins, this number can only be viewed as a conservative estimate. Today most Jews live in Warsaw, with smaller numbers in the cities of Wrocław, Cracow, Łódź, Szczecin, Gdańsk, and Katowice. There are virtually no Jews in the eastern parts of the country where large, historic, and important communities had once existed, such as those of Lublin, Białystok, and Przemyśl. But the number of Jews in Poland might be higher than assumed as a result of the growing "rediscovery" of Jewish ancestry among Poles who were either raised as Christians during the Holocaust or whose parents or grandparents hid their Jewish origins during the Nazi and Communist eras. Increasingly many such Poles with Jewish roots are joining the small but blossoming urban Jewish communities. This is especially true in Warsaw, where efforts have been taken to reestablish Jewish institutions in post-Communist Poland.

The Union of Jewish Religious Communities (*Związek Kongregacji Wyznania Mojzeszowego*), or *Kehillah*, and the secular Jewish Socio-Cultural Society (*Towarzystwo Społeczno-Kulturalne Żydów*), or *Ferband*, are the two major Jewish communal organizations which, together with other Jewish groups, are members of an umbrella organization, the Coordinating Committee of Jewish Organizations. They help provide the small but growing Jewish community an infrastructure to continue its development. Other important organizations include the Jewish Historical Institute, which opened its refurbished museum in June 2000; the E. R. Kaminska State Yiddish Theater in Warsaw, which remains one of the few regularly operating Yiddish theaters in the world; and the Jewish Cultural Center in Cracow. There are also centers for Jewish studies at Warsaw University and the Jagiellonian University in Cracow. While the Jewish Historical Institute serves a crucial function in documenting Polish Jewry's long and rich history, the Ronald S. Lauder Foundation of New York has sponsored a number of important activities throughout Central and Eastern Europe since its establishment in 1987, proving indispensable to the restoration of some semblance of Jewish life in Poland.

Since the Lauder-Morasha School was founded in a suburb of Warsaw in 1994 with funding from the Lauder Foundation—the first Jewish school in Poland in more than a quarter of a century—it grew significantly from an initial class of just eighteen students to well over a hundred. This spurred the school's relocation, after functioning for five years in a small house, to a restored five-story building near the wartime Warsaw Ghetto where thousands of Jews had perished during the Second World War. Prior to the Holocaust, the building had been a Jewish retirement home. The establishment of Warsaw's Jewish school was a defining moment in the reawakening of Jewish life on Polish soil.

In December 2000, Rabbi Schudrich arrived at New York's Ezra Academy Jewish Day School in Woodbridge to bless a 120-year-old restored Torah scroll, itself a survivor of the Holocaust. The school had donated it to the Lauder-Morasha School in Warsaw, which lacked its own Torah.[2] Rich in symbolism, this ceremony confirmed the genuine growth in Warsaw's contemporary Jewish cultural and religious awareness in the decade following the end of Communist rule in Poland.

Warsaw's synagogue was the victim of an apparent arson attack in February 1997; this was perceived as a setback for those pessimistic that Jewish life could ever again thrive in Poland. What the future holds for Polish Jews remains to be seen, however, as does the sincerity of Catholic Poles' recognition, appreciation, and acceptance of Jewish civilization as a vital part of their nation's history. After centuries of vibrant Jewish life in Poland all but ended with the devastation of the Holocaust, followed by the eviction of the majority of Poland's remaining Jews, it is not expected that Poland will ever again reclaim its place as the center of world Jewish culture. But the modest hints of its resurgence in Poland's youthful democracy are encouraging signs that it will not entirely disappear from the land where it thrived for close to a millennium.

❧

The 1997 Polish constitution not only reaffirmed the Third Republic as a democratic state ruled by law with a system of government that rests on the principle of the separation and balance of powers, but it also articulated the inherent, inalienable, and inviolable dignity of its inhabitants as a source of rights and freedoms. These constitutional provisions served as a major advance in Poland's quest to become an influential modern European state. However, as stated earlier, Poles need to come to terms with the notorious period of 1967–68 in order for Poland to move forward as a progressive nation in the new Europe. Moreover, unless contemporary Polish leaders publicly confront the errors of their predecessors to avoid repeating them, Poland's future remains uncertain.

Recent efforts in this direction provide reason for optimism.

In August 2000 an extraordinary gesture occurred. Leaders of Poland's Roman Catholic Church asked forgiveness for the Church's toleration of anti-Semitism and contempt of non-Catholics. Poland's bishops had approved a letter of joint apologies for failings in the Church's history at a special Jubilee Year session at Poland's holiest shrine of Jasna Góra in Częstochowa. Parish priests across Poland were instructed to read the letter during Sunday Mass, a significant act since nearly 96 percent of Poles identify themselves as Roman Catholics.[3] Likewise, President Kwaśniewski has also taken encouraging steps to address past misdeeds, including the commemoration of the wartime massacre of Jews at Jedwabne and the return of Polish citizenship to Poles of Jewish descent who had been sent off into exile.

Considering that only a small fraction of Poland's Jews survived the Holocaust, and that many of those who did were subsequently driven out by the Communist government's 1967–68 anti-Semitic propaganda campaign, Poles in the future could conceivably forget about the many significant Jewish contributions to Polish civilization. After all, before the Second World War Poland had 3.3 million Jews, a figure that not only represented 10 percent of Poland's population, but also represented the largest Jewish population of any country in Europe. National memory loss would therefore prove a distressing prospect for both Jewish and Polish civilization. However, there is evidence that this situation might be redressed.

An increasing number of Poles, particularly among the younger generation, has revealed a curious interest in Jewish themes. Many appear to understand that the Jewish people were indeed a part of the Polish setting for centuries, and further realize that this important piece of the Polish historical experience is painfully absent today. At one extreme, observes theologian Byron L. Sherwin, "Some young Poles also hold a romanticized view of Jews, much like some Americans imagine that Indians enjoyed an idyllic existence in the centuries prior to European settlement of the Americas." Even so, many Poles appear eager to fill in the "blank spots" of their history and of their nation's identity, which is encouraging. The importance of the Jewish issue in a country virtually empty of Jews, suggests Sherwin, "seems to have more to do with the reconceptualization of Polish identity in the post-communist era than it has to do with an attempt by Poles to recover the lost heritage of Polish Jews."[4] Still, this may ultimately prove beneficial if it enables Poles to look at their past through wider lenses.

As Poles reformulate their identity in the post-Communist era, education—whether obtained formally in school classrooms or informally via governmental public awareness programs—will help Poles learn about their nation's complex past and the ingredients that made it unique. Greater appreciation of the significance of Jews in Polish history should be among the identified outcomes, thereby enabling Poles to reclaim "lost" history as part of their nation's identity. Surveys have shown that Polish children in post-Communist Poland know very little about Jews in general or Polish Jews in particular.[5] Measures being taken to reverse this downward trend should be encouraged. In recognition that much of the world's richest Jewish culture emerged from Poland, plans have been drawn up, with the Polish government's support, for the construction of an impressive multimillion dollar interactive Museum of the History of Polish Jews in the heart of the former Warsaw Ghetto. Designed by Canadian-born American architect Frank Gehry, son of Jews who left Poland before the Second World War, the museum will contain exhibits from an electronic archive of documents, family photographs, and official registers from Poland's former Jewish communities; historians have spent several years putting it together.

The inspiration for the museum emerged, in part, from considerable soul-searching among Poland's leadership following the recent renewed attention, discussions, and inquiries into what took place in the town of Jedwabne during the war. For contemporary Poles to be reminded that Polish villagers, rather than the occupying Nazis, killed the Jewish residents of this town has proven troubling for many. According to Jerzy Halbersztadt, a historian named director of the museum project, much "has changed in the knowledge and attitudes of Jews towards Poles and Poles towards Jews," but this mainly has been "limited to the elites. What is needed is mass education, and in my opinion it is needed on both sides."[6] A balanced educational program is indeed essential for understanding past—and prevention of future—Jewish persecution. If these desired objectives are achieved, then the new Warsaw museum will have proven to be a worthy investment to tangibly illustrate that for close to a millennium, Poland had been a vibrant center of Jewish culture.

The museum will be a place where young, impressionable Polish students can learn about an important aspect of their nation's history. However, other efforts—much like Roman Polański's film *The Pianist*—are still needed to show that some shred of Jewish life and Polish decency survived the Second World War. Ensuring that this trend of mutual understanding and toleration continues will enable Poland's contemporary Jewish community to continue its growth in the future.

Post-Communist Poland and its Place in the New Europe

At the dawn of the third millennium, Poland must determine how to preserve its identity within a Europe once again undergoing rapid change. Although Polish history has shown that loss of political power does not necessarily equal loss of a vibrant culture or national yearnings—as the period between 1795 and 1918 proved—there is little doubt that loss of political power hampers the continuous development of cultural achievements and certainly harms morale among those who identify exclusively with that culture. Will the positive changes in Poland's post-1989, post-Communist era endure? Optimism is appropriate given Poland's membership in the European Union, but considering the precedents of history there is no certain answer.

It must not be forgotten that by the sixteenth-century reign of King Sigismund II Augustus, the last ruler of the Jagiellonian dynasty, Poland had become one of the richest and most powerful states on the European continent, stretching all the way from the Baltic Sea to the Black Sea. Moreover, two centuries later on 3 May 1791, the Polish-Lithuanian Commonwealth had ratified a constitution—not a whimsical elusive document, but the first written constitution in Europe. Despite these admirable achievements, just four years later Poland was partitioned among its inhospitable neighbors, and ceased to exist as a state for 123 years. Though Poland regained its independence in 1918, this autonomy lasted for only two decades when war again consumed Europe.

With the failure of the postwar Communist experiment, it is possible that the power and identity of the modern Polish state will once again be threatened as a result of joining the European Union, a large and powerful economic and political bloc. For its political and cultural independence to be preserved, therefore, it is imperative that Poland safeguards its unique identity by keeping its history, achievements, and culture alive in the minds of its inhabitants. This includes respecting and embracing Jewish culture as part of Poland's rich multiethnic past.

᚜᚜

When the plan for Europe's future was established by 1992's Maastricht Treaty, the result pointed toward a European Union with common citizenship, common defense and foreign policies, and a common currency, with many laws enacted by a European Parliament rather than merely national parliaments. Additionally considered was a more equitable distribution of wealth benefiting the poorer countries in the south, such as Spain, as well as those countries of the former Eastern Bloc, notably Poland. Maastricht proved a highly significant milestone in determining the future of Europe.

As Poland joined the EU in 2004, it became a member of an expanding alliance that possesses the potential to improve Poland's economic situation while bringing it more solidly into the Western sphere of influence.[7] This process began at a very quick pace after Poland's acceptance of democratic principles following the massive upheaval of 1989 and its subsequent membership in NATO, the Western defense organization, which for years had been Poland's sworn enemy in accordance with Soviet dictates.

In order to prevent Poland's cultural decline inside the EU, Poles will have to develop and maintain a strong understanding and appreciation of their national identity, language, culture, and position in Europe, particularly once Poles start to migrate in significant numbers throughout the EU as Poland eventually gains full rights. Once substantial migration occurs, more Poles will be exposed to other cultures, languages, and histories. Without a solid understanding of Poland's unique historic pluralistic identity, however, Poles will find it difficult to successfully adapt to change, appreciate the importance and legitimacy of human rights and ethnic diversity, and sustain positive economic, political, or even military cooperation with other nations.

Recognizing trends in Polish history will help Poles understand the challenges of maintaining a distinct cultural identity within an often-changing Europe. Given a history marked by a cycle of growth, decline, and resurgence, however, Poles might feel skeptical that change can ever be both positive and enduring. This attitude should evolve so that Poland, as an established EU member, can progress and compete on the same playing field as other nations. After all, Poles will not be fighting against their European neighbors over territory or fighting minority groups within; they must work together with other nations and fellow Polish citizens to build a better nation and a better Europe for all member states.

Poland's Historic Strength—Multiculturalism

Whether it comes to specific policy development or the adoption of a common currency, for Poland's political and cultural independence to be protected within the EU, it is imperative that Poland preserves its unique identity while respecting and accommodating the needs and interests of its minorities. In this way, Poland will not only become stronger politically and economically, but also culturally.

Rather than follow the path of an isolated, insular, xenophobic nation—a route taken after the Second World War when Poland became ethnically and nationally homogenous—Poland should emulate the principles that once made it so powerful and sophisticated prior to its eighteenth-century partition—its multicultural heritage as cultivated during the Polish-Lithuanian Commonwealth, when Poland was a conglomerate of peoples of different nationalities, cultures, and religions.

Recounting the significance of pre-partitioned Poland, Norman Davies writes, "Within the confines of the old Republic, there flourished a profusion of peoples, a riot of religions, a luxuriance of languages," which stimulated Poland's development and identity formation. "The cultural variety of old Polish society encouraged a number of specific attitudes," including preparing the ground for "practical toleration," promoting a cultural environment of "cross-fertilization where open-minded people could learn from their neighbours; and it encouraged a strong tradition of education, where each of the communities had to emulate the others in the excellence of their schools and academies."[8] Indeed, within the once vast Polish-Lithuanian state it was common to hear people speaking Polish, Yiddish, Ukrainian, Lithuanian, Belorussian, and German, as well as numerous regional dialects, and to see Catholics, Jews, Eastern Orthodox, Protestants, and even Muslims living side by side. Marked by peaceful coexistence and occasional conflict, the multicultural character that took shape not only helped stimulate Poland's economic and cultural development, but also ultimately helped encourage among Poles an appreciation of other cultures as part and parcel of their own.

It was not uncommon for Polish nobles in the sixteenth century to go abroad to learn from other cultures and then return home to refine those ideas within the Polish environment. As mentioned in chapter 1, Prince Radziwill had done just that, leading to his legendary fortuitous meeting in Italy with Rabbi Katzenellenbogen.

This practice continued among members of the Polish intelligentsia during the nineteenth century. Toward the end of that century, however, when Polish politicians began dreaming of restoring a Polish nation state, different opinions were articulated concerning which model this future independent Polish nation should be based on.

Rather than Józef Piłsudski and his Polish Socialist Party's vision of the multicultural and sophisticated "Jagiellonian" concept, other ideas prevailed, like those espoused by peasant leaders led by Bolesław Wysłouch and the nationalists led by Roman Dmowski, founder of *Endecja.* Motivated by supposed ideals of "ethnic purity," they latched onto the ancient state of the early Piasts as the type of Poland that they wanted to create in a modern form—the Poland of Mieszko I and Bolesław I, the Brave. The kind of Poland, in Davies's words, "of the early Polish tribes as yet undiluted by German colonists, Jewish refugees, or Ruthenian conquests; the Poland of their ancestors whom, it was claimed, held absolute right of possession to their Polish land."[9] While this vision of Poland may have been easier to cultivate because of its narrower focus, in the long run it may prove detrimental to Poland's success in the ethnically diverse EU, where a feeling of ease among different cultures will prove economically and politically essential. This is certainly true if Poland desires to play a greater role on the world stage.

For precedents, Poland need look no further than its own history when Jewish life, culture, and intellectual endeavors were developing throughout the Polish realm. Describing Jewish-Polish progress as an important outgrowth of its mutual geographical, intellectual, and social evolution, Poland's historical lands rather than the current borders of the Republic of Poland established after the Second World War represent what Sherwin vividly describes as "the boundaries both of Polish history and culture, and of the social and spiritual heritage of Polish Jewry."[10] Therefore, while Cracow, Lublin, Poznań, Warsaw, and Białystok remain within the borders of the Third Republic of Poland, leading centers of Polish Jewry include former great Polish cities that have since been absorbed by other countries, yet contribute to Polish and Jewish cultural identities.

At the height of its power, Poland ruled over a vast expanse of Eastern Europe. Part of Polish Jewry's legacy therefore exists in the culture and scholarship developed in the prominent city of Lemberg in Galicia—known as Lwów under Polish rule, Lvov under Soviet control, now Lviv inside the Ukraine—a region where Hasidism blossomed in the eighteenth century. There are cities and villages in contemporary Lithuania, such as Vilnius (Wilno during Polish rule, or Vilna in Yiddish), where the Jewish opponents of Hasidism flourished. In Byelorussia (Belarus) were the cities of Minsk, with its Jewish population of 90 percent, and Vitebsk (Witebsk in Polish), the birthplace of painter Marc Chagall. In between Belarus and Lithuania was Podlasie, where Jews populated such towns as Grodno (now within Belarus). In the north the Kingdom of Poland-Lithuania stretched far beyond Wilno. In the east, it bordered on the Muscovite kingdom. In the west, Poznań (Posen in German) was near Poland's western frontier with the German lands.[11]

During the period of Poland's greatest geographical and intellectual growth, particularly the era of the Jagiellonian dynasty and afterwards, the Jews of Poland experienced substantial political, intellectual, and social achievements that should be viewed in a favorable light not only by Poles, but also by others who consider Poland a positive example of early multicultural success. Only by embracing the strong, collective identity of its once large multicultural nation can Poland thrive within the new Europe as a cohesive, progressive country respectful of human rights, democratic principles, and economic power. With its unique background and efforts to combat anti-Semitism in Polish society, Poland can serve as a model of tolerance for other EU members, as it is false to assume that the expansion of the European Union means anti-Semitism will spontaneously disappear on its own. What might seem true in theory is often refuted by reality. Thus, to believe that a strong, sophisticated EU implies the absence of anti-Semitism will inevitably give rise to a false sense of security.

France, long considered a model of democracy and human rights, has seen an alarming rise in reported anti-Semitic incidents in recent years, reaching levels higher than anywhere else in contemporary Europe. Despite being among the largest members of the EU, France can still learn from other nations that have proactively chosen to deal with the social problem of anti-Semitism in a constructive way. Since the year 2000, France has been the site of hundreds of anti-Semitic incidents including vandalism of synagogues, destruction of sacred texts, and threats made to Jewish individuals. In the spring of 2003, France witnessed physical attacks against Jews at a rate of eight to twelve per day, with fourteen arson attacks on synagogues over a two-week period. Such statistics are startling. As Rudolph Giuliani, former mayor of New York City, wrote in the New York Times: "When people attack Jews, vandalize their graves, characterize them in inhumane ways, and make salacious statements in parliaments or the press, they are attacking the defining values of our societies and our international institutions."[12] President Jacques Chirac appears to have recognized the cause for alarm.

Because disaffected Muslim youths were alleged to have been behind most of the anti-Semitic acts in France in an ill-placed attempt to discharge their anger at events occurring in the Middle East, President Chirac called an emergency high-level meeting to approve measures to stop attacks on Jewish sites. Chirac pledged that the French government would try to prevent anti-Semitic acts by increasing police guards at Jewish institutions, assigning special magistrates to work more closely with Jewish community leaders, accelerate trials, and apply harsher penalties for those convicted of anti-Semitic acts. He also pledged billions of dollars for urban renewal in challenged areas with heavy Muslim populations.[13]

Following an arson attack that destroyed a Jewish school in Gagny, north of Paris, President Chirac told reporters, "Anti-Semitism is contrary to all the values of France," and stressed that Jews, having lived in French lands for centuries, "are at home in France, as is each and every one of our compatriots."[14] While France is certainly not alone in its fight against anti-Semitism—which has risen in a number of countries both inside and outside the EU as a result of ongoing challenges in the Middle East—Poland is in a position to show the world how acceptance of Jewish culture as part and parcel of its historic national culture strengthens, not weakens, its identity. In this way, the masses will be less inclined to tolerate prejudice and anti-Semitism, which if not entirely eliminated may prove more easily contained.

❧

Rather than focus narrowly on its early history when a more "ethnically pure" Poland existed during the Piast dynasty, Poland should acknowledge the significance of its multicultural past, including the once influential

Jewish community that thrived during the Jagiellonian period. Such conditions helped make Poland a powerful commonwealth, successfully achieving great economic and cultural progress. Poland should therefore look to the Jagiellonian era as a contemporary ideal. By emulating some of the more positive aspects of this age, Poles will be better prepared to accept the challenges to the nation's political sovereignty as a new EU member. They must accept that political power is not the only means to prosperity, but that in the current era, achieving broad cultural power while preserving state identity offers a position of considerably greater strength. It will also show other nations of the EU that anti-Semitism must be fought vigorously to dispel the notion that toleration of anti-Semitic attacks—or attacks on any minority—is acceptable.

Polish history is not stagnant but vibrant and, therefore, any profound change like entrance to the EU poses a significant challenge to Poles' sense of identity. Looking toward the future, Poles from all generations and economic and social strata must learn about the strengths of Poland's multicultural heritage. Not only will this serve to remind Poles of their nation's historic sources of strength and the variety of ingredients that contributed to Poland's cultural development over the centuries, but it will also enable them to realize that accommodations to the ideas of other nations within an EU framework need not be interpreted as a challenge to the continuation of a strong, vibrant Polish identity. Thus, within the structure of the European Union, Poland will be capable of retaining a strong national identity that is respectful of its pluralistic past and existing minorities.

The Lessons of History

Considering Poland's 1967-68 anti-Jewish campaign in context of the history of Jewish suffering in Poland and elsewhere, individuals throughout the world must be alert to the potential for similar developments in the future. In Machiavellian fashion, desperate regimes may reprise the theme of the Jew as convenient scapegoat. Mindful of this concern, Polish-born Pope John Paul II—speaking on the occasion of the fiftieth anniversary of the liberation of prisoners from Auschwitz—pleaded: "Never again anti-Semitism! Never again the arrogance of nationalism! Never again genocide! May the third millennium usher in a season of peace and mutual respect among peoples."[15]

Given the fearful prospect that such reprehensible events as those that occurred in 1967-68 could again someday take place in Poland, it is hoped that Poland's constitution, which even during the Communist period explicitly guaranteed the freedom of speech and press as well as the protection of minorities, will be upheld as sacrosanct. We know from what happened in Poland in the late 1960s that those guarantees were not worth the paper on which they were written. The reason they were not was because Polish authorities arbitrarily deemed the infringements of these rights as "reasonable" or "necessary" for the country's security needs at the time and the supposed greater good of the Polish people. Hopefully those who witnessed that kind of political cynicism and amoral political pragmatism will, in the post-Communist Poland of the New Europe, echo the wise words of the Polish-born pontiff and add "never again" to violations of the constitution as well.

Afterword

I didn't know any Jews, or at least I thought I didn't. No one had taught me their history or customs. Or pointed out how deeply rooted they were in this land that was mine. No one made me aware of the foundations of the centuries-long Polish-Jewish heritage.

— Agata Tuszyńska, *Lost Landscapes*

If Polish culture represents as strong a reflection of Polish identity as the possession of political power is perceived to do, then Poles have little need to worry. Despite some inevitable loss of political autonomy, maintaining a unique Polish identity within the European Union should not be perceived as a threat to Poles' sense of identity, nor to their political and cultural independence.

For centuries Polish culture has been a vital part of European culture. One need only consider names from a variety of fields to see the profound effect of Polish contributions to European culture: Astronomer Nicolas Copernicus, composer and pianist Fryderyk Chopin, and Nobel-Prize-winning scientist Marie Curie-Skłodowska are but a few. Author Joseph Conrad, whose original surname was Korzeniowski—a descendant of szlachta, Polish nobility—spent his formative years in Cracow before migrating to England and becoming one of the greatest modern stylists of English prose.

Even in more recent decades Polish culture has shown a strong influence on European culture. Not only has the

Nobel Prize for literature been awarded to Polish poets Czesław Miłosz and Wisława Szymborska, but other Nobel laureates also include Warsaw-born Isaac Bashevis Singer, whose Yiddish stories often involved the Jewish experience in Poland. Likewise, Nobel Laureate Shmuel Yosef Agnon, though living most of his life in Israel, was a native of Galicia, an important part of interwar Poland. His Hebrew writings, which earned him the esteemed Nobel Prize for literature, chronicled the decline of Jewish life in Galicia, where he spent his formative years.

Poland's long musical tradition has continued from Chopin through such influential composers and musicians as Henryk Wieniawski, Ignacy Paderewski, Artur Rubinstein, Krzysztof Penderecki, Henryk Górecki, Witold Łutosławski, and Władysław Szpilman, while films by Andrzej Wajda, Krzysztof Kieślowski, and Roman Polański have contributed significantly to European and international cinema. The point is not to provide an endless list of names, but to confirm that Polish culture has indeed made as profound an impact on Poland as it has on Europe and the world, just as Poland's Jewish presence has made a strong impact on Polish, European, and world culture notwithstanding centuries of oppression capped off by the Polish government's 1967-68 official anti-Semitic campaign.

Hints of popular anti-Semitism still pop up from time to time. While such disgraceful attitudes may never be entirely wiped out in Poland or from other nations where it has deep roots, the potential for the political form of anti-Semitism is reduced now that Poland has emerged from the oppressive rule of Communism. Popular anti-Semitic sentiments, however, must be vigorously fought to prevent the spread of ideas that can only harm citizens and the nation's reputation.

Many of Poland's most prominent cultural figures of Jewish descent, from Wieniawski, Rubinstein, and Szpilman to Polański and Bashevis Singer, plus innumerable scientists, intellectuals, philosophers, and a plethora of bakers, merchants, tailors, and farm workers of Jewish parentage, have had a profound and positive impact on Poland, Europe, and the world. This influence should be embraced and celebrated by Poles, not hidden, denied, condemned, or forgotten. Poland will be the better for it.

Jews who choose to reside in Poland today as *Jews*—who are neither ashamed nor fearful of their ethnic identity being known to their neighbors—will hopefully be able to do so within a climate of peace and without the fear that marked the Jewish people of Poland during the Communist era and in prior tumultuous decades. Education will indeed prove crucial for the Polish people's understanding of Poland's place in Europe, and the value of Poland's history and diverse ethnic heritage to creating a strong nation within a stable multicultural Europe.

If the 1967-68 campaign can teach the world one thing, it is that anti-Semitism never ends with the Jews; it only begins with them. Since hatred cannot be easily contained it must therefore be vigorously fought, for who knows who will become the next target? While it must always be remembered that in 1967-68 Polish Jews served as the scapegoat of a failing Communist regime, the significance of this fact must never be forgotten. In a future marked by similar or different circumstances, this unfortunate role could be filled by anyone.

Notes

Introduction

1. Paul Lendvai, *Anti-Semitism Without Jews: Communist Eastern Europe*, 1st ed. (Garden City, NY: Doubleday, 1971), 23.

2. Roman Polański's film *The Pianist* won the 2002 Golden Palm (*Palm d'Or*) at the Cannes Film Festival for best film and won numerous awards in 2003 at both the British Academy of Film and Television Arts Awards and the Academy Awards (Oscars), among numerous other awards received in countries across Europe, including Poland's own Polish Film Awards, which confirmed its broad international appeal.

3. Eva Hoffman, *Exit Into History: A Journey Through the New Eastern Europe* (New York: Penguin Books, 1993), 43.

4. For an explanation of why anti-Zionism equals Anti-Semitism, see Dennis Prager and Joseph Telushkin, *Why The Jews? The Reason For Antisemitism* (New York: Simon & Schuster, 1983), 170–75.

5. See Bernard Lewis, *Semites and Anti-Semites: An Inquiry into Conflict and Prejudice* (New York: Norton, 1986), 81.

Chapter 1

1. Abram Leon Sachar, *A History of The Jews*, 5th ed. (New York: Alfred A. Knopf, 1967), 223–24.

2. For a translation and discussion of "The Charter of the Jews of the Duchy of Austria July 1, 1244," see Jacob R. Marcus, *The Jew in the Medieval World: A Source Book, 315–1791* (New York: Macmillan, 1938), 28–33.

3. Sachar, *History of The Jews*, 224.

4. The "Polish" connection in Lithuania took on the same connotation as the "British" connection in Scotland. Poland's "Lithuanian connection" brought further enrichment to its already rich multinational heritage. See Norman Davies, *Heart of Europe: A Short History of Poland* (New York: Oxford University Press, 1986), 291–92.

5. Sachar, *History of The Jews*, 224–25.

6. The genealogy of Saul Wahl Katzenellenbogen has been extensively researched. His diverse list of descendants include such names as Karl Marx, the Jewish philosopher Moses Mendelssohn and his grandson, composer Felix Mendelssohn-Bartholdy, Jewish philosopher Martin Buber, and cosmetics entrepreneur Helena Rubenstein. For details on Saul Wahl's ancestors, descendents, and their achievements, see Neil Rosenstein, *The Unbroken Chain: Biographical Sketches and Genealogy of Illustrious Jewish Families from the 15th–20th Century* (Elizabeth, NJ: Computer Center for Jewish Genealogy, 1990), 2 vols. For a historical and personal account of Saul Wahl's achievements, see Byron L. Sherwin, *Sparks Amid the Ashes: The Spiritual Legacy of Polish Jewry* (New York: Oxford University Press, 1997), 68–78. Another account of the legendary Saul Wahl can be found in Gustav Karpeles, "A Jewish King in Poland" in *Jewish Literature and Other Essays* (Freeport, NY:

Books for Libraries Press, 1971), 272–92 (reprint of the 1895 edition).

7. For details of Saul Wahl Katzenellenbogen's legendary rise to the position of "King of Poland" for a night, see Rosenstein, *The Unbroken Chain*, Vol. 1, 5–9.

8. See Marcus, *The Jew in the Medieval World*, 205.

9. For a description of the evolving social and legal situation during the age of reforms and partition, see Raphael Mahler, *A History of Modern Jewry, 1780–1815* (New York: Schocken, 1971), 299–303.

10. Davies, *Heart of Europe*, 294–95.

11. Ibid., 296–97.

12. Norman Davies, *God's Playground: A History of Poland* (New York: Columbia University Press, 1982), vol. 1, 212–13.

13. Royal charters protected the separate legal positions of the clergy, the burghers, and the Jews, and therefore formed separate social estates while enjoying a broad measure of independence. For the most part they were exempt from direct noble control, but nobles formed only a small part of the population as a whole. Consequently, with the exception of the noble bishops in the Senate, they played little part in the institutions of Poland's central government. Still, their number was large by comparison with other European states. Where the nobility formed only 1 or 2 percent of society elsewhere, the Polish *szlachta* (the nobility) were very numerous at 8 to 12 percent and formed by a significant margin the largest franchised class in Europe. See Davies, *Heart of Europe*, 297–98.

14. Bruce F. Pauley, *From Prejudice to Persecution: A History of Austrian Anti-Semitism* (Chapel Hill and London: University of North Carolina Press, 1992), 22.

Chapter 2

1. Lionel Kochan, "East European Jewry since 1770," in David Englander, ed., *The Jewish Enigma* (New York: Braziller, 1992), 131.

2. Stephen J. Roth, "Anti-Zionism and Anti-Semitism in the USSR," in Theodore Freedman, ed., *Anti-Semitism in the Soviet Union: Its Roots and Consequences* (New York: Anti-Defamation League of B'nai B'rith, 1984), 160.

3. For a discussion of Poland's constitutional provisions, see William B. Simons, ed., *The Constitutions of the Communist World* (Germantown, MD: Sijthoff & Noordhoff, 1980), 283–310.

4. Celia Stopnicka Heller, "'Anti-Zionism' and the Political Struggle within the Elite of Poland," *Journal of Jewish Sociology* 11.2 (December 1969), 149.

5. See Adam Podgórecki, *Polish Society* (Westport, CT: Praeger, 1994), 81–84.

6. For a discussion of the complex origins of anti-Semitism, see Dennis Prager and Joseph Telushkin, *Why the Jews? The Reason for Antisemitism*, 20–26; and Philip S. Alexander, "The Origins of Religious and Racial Anti-Semitism and the Jewish Response," in *The Jewish Enigma*, ed. David Englander (New York: Braziller, 1992), 169–95.

7. See Michal Borwicz, "Polish-Jewish Relations, 1944–1947," in *The Jews in Poland*, ed. Chimen Abramsky, Maciej Jachimczyk, and Antony Polonsky (New York: Basil Blackwell, 1986), 193.

8. For a detailed account of the Jedwabne massacre, postwar trials, and verdicts, see Jan T. Gross, *Neighbors: The Destruction of the Community of Jedwabne, Poland* (Princeton, NJ: Princeton University Press, 2001).

9. In 2001, following the end of another official investigation into Jedwabne, President Aleksander

Kwaśniewski, the democratically elected leader of Poland's post-Communist government, visited the Polish town to deliver a public apology—for what Poles of one faith did to Poles of another—to help improve relations between Poland's Christians and Jews at a ceremony marking the sixtieth anniversary of the pogrom.

10. See Robert S. Wistrich, *Antisemitism: The Longest Hatred* (New York: Schocken, 1991), 176–78.

11. See Tadeusz Szafar, "Anti-Semitism: A Trusty Weapon," in *Poland: Genesis of a Revolution*, ed. Abraham Brumberg (New York: Random House, 1983), 110–11.

12. Michael R. Marrus, *The Holocaust in History* (Toronto: Lester & Orpen Dennys, 1987), 96.

13. Keith Sword, *Deportation and Exile: Poles in the Soviet Union, 1939–48* (London: Macmillan, 1994), 195.

14. Szafar, "Anti-Semitism: A Trusty Weapon," 110.

15. Jan B. de Weydenthal, *The Communists of Poland: An Historical Outline* (Stanford, CA: Hoover Institution Press, 1986), 129.

16. Martin Myant, *Poland: A Crisis for Socialism* (London: Lawrence and Wishart, 1982), 43–46.

17. Konrad Syrop, *Poland in Perspective* (London: Robert Hale, 1982), 191–92.

Chapter 3

1. J. B. Schechtman, "The USSR, Zionism, and Israel," in *The Jews in Soviet Russia Since 1917*, 3rd ed., ed. Lionel Kochan (New York: Oxford University Press, 1978), 130–31.

2. Zev Katz, "After the Six-Day War," in *The Jews in Soviet Russia Since 1917*, 3rd ed., ed. Lionel Kochan (New York: Oxford University Press, 1978), 334.

3. Bernard D. Weinryb, "Antisemitism in Soviet Russia," in *The Jews in Soviet Russia Since 1917*, 3rd ed., ed.

Lionel Kochan (New York: Oxford University Press, 1978), 327.

4. Institute of Jewish Affairs, *Anti-Jewish Campaign in Present-Day Poland: Facts, Documents, Press Reports*, 2nd ed. (London, 1968), 11.

5. Wistrich, *Antisemitism*, 162.

6. Leonard B. Schapiro, "Antisemitism in the Communist World," *Soviet Jewish Affairs* 9.1 (1979), 49–50.

7. Although Romania did not experience Poland's official anti-Semitism in 1968, a similar strategy of "calculated anti-Semitism" was employed by Romania in the 1980s. According to Leon Volovici, head of research at Hebrew University's Vidal Sassoon International Center of the Study of Antisemitism, "It's a tool which every political communist leader preserved in order to use when necessary. Because it works—or they are convinced that it works. But sometimes the reaction is the opposite, as in the same period in Poland." See Ky Krauthamer, "Imaginary Jews and Real Anti-Semites: An Interview with Leon Volovici," *Central Europe Review*, Vol. 4, No. 5, 15 November 2002, www.ce-review.org02/5aCER-VoloviciJB.html.

8. Kochan, "East European Jewry Since 1770," 136.

9. Michael Chęciński, *Poland: Communism, Nationalism, Anti-Semitism* (New York: Karz-Cohl Publishing, 1982), 241.

10. Nicholas Bethell, *Gomułka: His Poland and His Communism* (London: Penguin Books, 1972), 255.

11. Alfred D. Low, *Soviet Jewry and Soviet Policy* (New York: Columbia University Press, 1990), 100.

12. Lester Samuel Eckman, *Soviet Policy Towards Jews and Israel: 1917–1974* (New York: Shengold, 1974), 81.

13. Umberto Terracini, "Israel as a Factor in Soviet Anti-Semitism," in *Anti-Semitism in the Soviet Union: Its*

Roots and Consequences, ed. Theodore Freedman (New York: Anti-Defamation League of B'nai B'rith, 1984), 168.

14. See Schechtman, "The USSR, Zionism, and Israel," 128–30.

15. Arieh Tartakower, "The Jewish Problem in the Soviet Union," *Jewish Social Studies* 33.4 (October 1971), 301.

16. Louis Rapoport, *Stalin's War Against the Jews: The Doctors' Plot and the Soviet Solution* (New York: Free Press, 1990), 104.

Chapter 4

1. M. K. Dziewanowski, *The Communist Party of Poland: An Outline of History,* 2nd ed. (Cambridge, MA: Harvard University Press, 1976), 292–93.

2. Ibid., 293.

3. Jerzy Ptakowski, "Behind the Unrest in Poland," *East Europe* 17.4 (1968), 5–6.

4. For a detailed account of this group in Polish society, see Leszek Kołakowski, "The Intelligentsia," in *Poland: Genesis of a Revolution,* ed. Abraham Brumberg (New York: Random House, 1983), 54.

5. Ray Taras, Poland: *Socialist State, Rebellious Nation* (Boulder, CO: Westview Press, 1991), 139.

6. Jan Nowak, "Conflict of Generations in Poland," *East Europe* 17.5 (1968), 14.

7. See Syrop, *Poland in Perspective,* 191.

8. Josef Banas, *The Scapegoats: The Exodus of the Remnants of Polish Jewry,* trans. Tadeusz Szafar, ed. Lionel Kochan (London: Weidenfeld and Nicolson, 1979), 111.

9. George H. Mond, "The Student Rebels in Poland," *East Europe* 18.7 (1969), 3.

10. Nowak, "Conflict of Generations in Poland," 16.

11. Jerzy Ptakowski, "Gomulka and His Party," *East Europe* 16.5 (1967), 6.

12. For details of the survey, see Taras, *Poland*, 139–40.

13. Davies, *Heart of Europe*, 10–11.

14. Jerzy Eisler, "March 1968 in Poland," in *1968: The World Transformed*, ed. Carole Fink, Philipp Gassert, and Detlef Junker (Cambridge, UK: Cambridge University Press, 1998), 246.

15. See R. Brasch, *How Did It Begin? Customs, Superstitions, and their Romantic Origins* (Sydney, Australia: HarperCollins, 1993), 187–88.

16. de Weydenthal, *Communists of Poland*, 134–35.

17. Bauman's ideas are quoted in Banas, *The Scapegoats*, 149–50.

18. For an analysis of the origins and development of Jew-hatred, see Howard M. Sachar, *The Course of Modern Jewish History*, 3rd ed., rev. (New York: Random House, 1990), 255–57.

19. See Frank Golczewski, "Rural Anti-Semitism in Galicia Before World War I," in *The Jews in Poland*, ed. Chimen Abramsky, Maciej Jachimczyk, and Antony Polonsky (Oxford: Basil Blackwell, 1986), 100–1.

20. Neal Ascherson, *The Struggles for Poland* (London: Michael Joseph, 1987), 174.

21. Ptakowski, "Behind the Unrest in Poland," 8.

22. Stewart Steven, *The Poles* (New York: Macmillan, 1982), 227.

Chapter 5

1. Bethell, *Gomułka*, 260.

2. Krystyna Kersten, *The Establishment of Communist Rule in Poland, 1943–1948*, trans. John Micgiel and

Michael H. Bernhard (Berkeley, CA: University of California Press, 1991), 451–52.

3. See "Mieczysław Moczar: Polish partisan leader sought supreme power," *The Globe and Mail* (Toronto), 3 November 1986, A16.

4. Jan Nowak, "The Struggle for Party Control in Poland," *East Europe* 17.6 (1968), 3.

5. Neal Ascherson, *The Polish August: The Self-Limiting Revolution* (London: Penguin, 1981), 90.

6. Steven, *The Poles*, 227.

7. Ascherson, *The Struggles for Poland*, 174.

8. Erwin Weit, *Eyewitness: The Autobiography of Gomułka's Interpreter*, trans. Mary Schofield (London: Andre Deutsch, 1973), 93.

9. Lendvai, *Anti-Semitism Without Jews*, 229–30.

10. Chęciński, *Poland*, 161.

11. Dziewanowski, *Communist Party of Poland*, 291–92.

12. Chęciński, 163–64.

13. Banas, *The Scapegoats*, 52.

14. Chęciński, 166.

15. Banas, 90.

16. Lendvai, 126.

17. Syrop, 196.

18. Ptakowski, "Behind the Unrest in Poland," 8.

19. Lewis, *Semites and Anti-Semites*, 36.

20. "Student Demonstrations in Poland," *East Europe* 17.4 (1968), 4.

21. Peter Raina, *Political Opposition in Poland: 1954–1977* (London: Poets and Painters Press, 1978), 133–34.

22. Teresa Torańska, *"Them": Stalin's Polish Puppets*, trans. Agnieszka Kolakowska (New York: Harper & Row, 1987), 88.

23. Concerning Adam Michnik's family background, his father was Ozjasj Szechter but Adam, born shortly after the War's end, went by his mother's maiden name, Michnik. Although his father was Jewish and his mother was not, Adam had always regarded himself as a Jew even though traditional Judaism ascribes one's Jewish status to having a Jewish mother, or through conversion to the Jewish faith by a rabbi (the modern Reform movement accepts one born of a Jewish father to be a Jew). Adam's father was from Lwów (Lvov), an important city in Poland prior to World War II—with a large Jewish population liquidated by the German occupiers—now part of the Ukraine, where the Nazis murdered ninety members of his family, including Adam's paternal grandparents. Following the war, Michnik was raised in an assimilated manner due to the prevailing anti-Jewish prejudice. As New York Times writer Roger Cohen asserts, "in Stalinist postwar Poland, official history had no place for the Holocaust." See Roger Cohen, "The Accommodations of Adam Michnik," *New York Times Magazine* (7 November 1999), 88.

24. Nowak, "Conflict of Generations in Poland," 16.

25. Bethell, 260.

26. Dziewanowski, *Communist Party*, 298.

27. An English translation of Gomułka's speech can be found in a number of publications. For another version, complete with vocal reactions of the audience, see Institute of Jewish Affairs, *Anti-Jewish Campaign in Present-Day Poland*, 30–32.

28. For the entire text, see Władysław Gomułka, "On Zionism," in *Poland Since 1956: Readings and Essays on Polish Government and Politics*, ed. Tadeusz N. Cieplak (New York: Twayne, 1972), 399–401.

29. Jakub Karpiński, *Countdown: The Polish Upheavals of 1956, 1968, 1970, 1976, 1980*, trans. Olga Amster-

damska and Gene M. Moore (New York: Karz-Cohl, 1982), 129.

30. Syrop, 196–97.

31. Eisler, "March 1968 in Poland," 249.

Chapter 6

1. Lewis, 19.

2. Bernard Wasserstein, *Vanishing Diaspora: The Jews in Europe Since 1945* (New York: Penguin, 1997), 212.

3. Tartakower, "The Jewish Problem in the Soviet Union," 287.

4. Eckman, *Soviet Policy Towards Jews and Israel*, 29, 31–32.

5. Shmuel Ettinger, "Historical and Internal Political Factors in Soviet Anti-Semitism," in *Anti-Semitism in the Soviet Union: Its Roots and Consequences*, ed. Theodore Freedman (New York: Anti-Defamation League of B'nai B'rith, 1984), 174.

6. See in particular Alex de Jonge, *Stalin, and the Shaping of the Soviet Union* (New York: William Morrow, 1986), 53, 65, 450, 475–78.

7. See Low, *Soviet Jewry and Soviet Policy*, 70, 97–99.

8. Ibid., 102.

9. Jonathan Kaufman, *A Hole in the Heart of the World: The Jewish Experience in Eastern Europe After World War II* (New York: Penguin, 1998), 108.

10. Sachar, *Course of Modern Jewish History*, 335–37. For an extended discussion of the historical growth of Jewish socialism and its effects on Jews in Europe and Russia, see 332–58.

11. See Maurice Friedberg, "Antisemitism as a Policy Tool in the Soviet Bloc," in *American Jewish Year Book: 1970*, ed. Morris Fine and Milton Himmelfarb (New York: The American Jewish Committee, 1971), 123–34.

12. Chęciński, 31.

13. Low, 100.

14. Friedberg, "Antisemitism as a Policy Tool in the Soviet Bloc," 124–25.

15. While the term "revisionist" was applied to those opposed to traditional Communist orthodoxy, the term was also used to imply a citizen with pro-Israeli sentiments. The reference was to the pre-World War II movement of Revisionist Zionism, led by Ze'ev (Vladimir) Jabotinsky. Gaining hundreds of thousands of supporters in Poland in the late 1920s and '30s, especially among Jewish youth, it prepared them for migration to then British-ruled Palestine. As a result, thousands of Polish Zionists immigrated to Palestine to help settle the land. Many later fought, together with postwar Jewish immigrants, to help create the State of Israel.

16. William Korey, "The Legal Position of Soviet Jewry: A Historical Enquiry," in *The Jews in Soviet Russia Since 1917*, 3rd ed., ed. Lionel Kochan (New York: Oxford University Press, 1978), 92–94, 99.

17. Low, 110.

18. Syrop, 193.

19. Ascherson, *The Struggles for Poland*, 174.

20. Quoted in Institute of Jewish Affairs, 39.

21. de Weydenthal, 130.

22. Since Poland's political reorganization into the People's Republic of Poland (1952–1989), following eight years of Communist transformation under the leadership of Bolesław Bierut, the ruling "Council of State" was in theory a collective head of state with a presiding president. However, the most important and powerful person in the Polish administration was the first secretary of the Central Committee of the Polish United Workers Party (PUWP). This key role was held by Bolesław Bierut (1948–1956), Edward Ochab (1956), Władysław

Gomułka (1956–1970), Edward Gierek (1970–1980), Stanisław Kania (1980–1981), and Wojciech Jaruzelski (1981–1989).

23. M. K. Dziewanowski, *Poland in the Twentieth Century* (New York: Columbia University Press, 1977), 203.

24. Christopher Cviic, "The Church," in *Poland: Genesis of a Revolution*, ed. Abraham Brumberg (New York: Random House, 1983), 93.

25. See Bogdan Szajkowski, *Next to God... Poland: Politics and Religion in Contemporary Poland* (London: Frances Pinter, 1983), 2–3, and Davies, *Heart of Europe*, 11.

26. Cviic, "The Church," 95.

27. Steven, 164–65.

28. Szajkowski, *Next to God*, 20.

29. Ibid., 22.

30. Cviic, 99.

31. Steven, 162.

Chapter 7

1. See Institute of Jewish Affairs, 6.

2. Oscar Halecki, *A History of Poland* (New York: Dorset, 1992), 326–27.

3. For a discussion of the situation in Poland immediately following the end of World War II, see Martin Gilbert, *The Day The War Ended* (London: HarperCollins, 1995), 238–42.

4. Václav L. Beneš and Norman John Greville Pounds, *Poland* (London: Ernest Benn, 1970), 261.

5. Louis Rapoport, *Stalin's War Against the Jews*, 176–77.

6. Eckman, 40.

7. Claiborne Pell, "The Pattern of Soviet Anti-Semitism," *East Europe* 20.3 (1971), 19.

8. Wasserstein, *Vanishing Diaspora*, 215–16.

9. Lendvai, 176.

10. Ibid., 177–78.

11. For statistics on the number of Jews who left Poland between 1968 and 1972, see Wasserstein, 215–16.

12. "Revisionist" referred to those who held progressive ideas contrary to Poland's Communist orthodoxy, as well as those who allegedly harbored pro-Zionist ideas deemed contrary to existing Communist dogma.

13. Sachar, *Course of Modern Jewish History*, 601–602.

14. Banas, 132.

15. Raina, *Political Opposition in Poland*, 169.

16. See Reuben Ainsztein, *Jewish Resistance in Nazi-Occupied Eastern Europe: With a Historical Survey of the Jew as Fighter and Soldier in the Diaspora* (New York: Barnes & Noble, 1975), 392.

17. Józef Parnas, *Sylwetki Moich Nauczycieli [Profiles of My Teachers]* (Copenhagen, Denmark: Kronika, 1984), 31.

18. Chęciński, 220.

19. Banas, 162.

20. Raina, 168–70.

21. Chęciński, 220.

22. Raina, 171.

23. Wistrich, 163.

24. Quoted in Ibid., 292.

25. See Raina, 171.

26. Ibid., 173.

27. After immigrating to Denmark, Dr. Parnas, in a publication of Radio Free Europe, thanked Dr. Edward Wolak, among other colleagues, scientists, representatives of the American Civil Liberties Union, and Amnesty International, who had worked tirelessly for years to secure his release. See Józef Parnas, "Spózniony

List z Więzienia" ["Belated Letter from Prison"], *Na
Antenie [On the Air]* 10.1 (September 1972), 2.
   28. Chęciński, 220.
   29. Józef Parnas, "Spózniony List z Więzienia"
["Belated Letter from Prison"], 2.

Chapter 8

   1. Syrop, 198–99.
   2. Lendvai, 94.
   3. Krystyna Kersten, *The Establishment of Communist
Rule in Poland,* 215.
   4. See Lonnie R. Johnson, *Central Europe: Enemies,
Neighbors, Friends* (New York: Oxford University Press,
1996), 260–61.
   5. Ibid., 260.
   6. Szajkowski, 30.
   7. See Vincent C. Chrypiński, "Political Change
Under Gierek," in *Gierek's Poland,* ed. Adam Bromke and
John W. Strong (New York: Praeger, 1973), 37.
   8. See "Rehabilitacja Józefa Parnasa" ["The Rehabilitation of Józef Parnas"], *Gazeta w Lublinie* (Thursday, 7
November 1991).
   9. See Marilyn Henry, "Poland to Expedite Citizenship for 'March' Victims," *Jerusalem Post* (11 March
1998), 5.
   10. Wasserstein, 216–17.
   11. Szafar, 120–21.
   12. Wasserstein, 217.

Chapter 9

   1. The estimate of the Jewish population in Poland is
based on statistics in *American Jewish Year Book 1996,* ed.
David Singer (New York: American Jewish Committee,

1997). Other sources report slightly higher figures. See Wasserstein, viii, who estimates the number of Jews in Poland at five thousand as of 1996.

2. Richard Weizel, "Donating a Torah to a Warsaw School," *New York Times* (14 January 2001), 14CN.2.

3. See "Catholics of Poland Apologize to Jews," *New York Times* (28 August 2000), A3.

4. Sherwin, *Sparks Amid The Ashes*, 136.

5. See Agata Tuszyńska, *Lost Landscapes: In Search of Isaac Bashevis Singer and the Jews of Poland*, trans. Madeline G. Levine (New York: William Morrow, 1998), 94–98.

6. Quoted in Peter S. Green, "Jewish Museum in Poland: More Than a Memorial," *New York Times* (9 January 2003), A3.

7. See "Poland and the European Union: Back into the Fold," *The Economist* (12 June 2003); and "A Nervous New Arrival on the European Union's Block," *The Economist* (28 August 2003).

8. Davies, *Heart of Europe*, 316–17.

9. See Ibid., 133, 323–26.

10. Sherwin, 69.

11. For details on the historical lands of Poland, see Davies, *God's Playground*, 23–60.

12. Rudolph W. Giuliani, "How Europe Can Stop the Hate," *New York Times* (18 June 2003), A25.

13. John Tagliabue, "Chirac to Tackle Anti-Semitism and Muslim Slums of Bitterness," *New York Times* (18 November 2003), A3.

14. Quoted in Ibid.

15. Pope John Paul II, *Spiritual Pilgrimage: Texts on Jews and Judaism, 1979–1995*, ed. Eugene J. Fisher and Leon Klenicki (New York: Crossroad, 1995), 209.

Bibliography

Ainsztein, Reuben. *Jewish Resistance in Nazi-Occupied Eastern Europe: With a Historical Survey of the Jew as Fighter and Soldier in the Diaspora.* New York: Barnes & Noble, 1975.

Alexander, Philip S. "The Origins of Religious and Racial Anti-Semitism and the Jewish Response." In *The Jewish Enigma,* edited by David Englander, 169–195. New York: Braziller, 1992.

Ascherson, Neal. *The Polish August: The Self-Limiting Revolution.* London: Penguin, 1981.

————. *The Struggles for Poland.* London: Michael Joseph, 1987.

Banas, Josef. *The Scapegoats: The Exodus of the Remnants of Polish Jewry.* Edited by Lionel Kochan. Translated by Tadeusz Szafar. London: Weidenfeld and Nicolson, 1979.

Beneš, Václav L., and Norman John Greville Pounds. *Poland.* London: Ernest Benn, 1970.

Bethell, Nicholas. *Gomułka: His Poland and His Communism.* London: Penguin Books, 1972.

Borwicz, Michal. "Polish-Jewish Relations, 1944–1947." In *The Jews in Poland*, edited by Chimen Abramsky, Maciej Jachimczyk, and Antony Polonsky, 190–198. Oxford and New York: Basil Blackwell, 1986.

Brasch, R. *How Did It Begin? Customs, Superstitions, and Their Romantic Origins.* Sydney, Australia: Harper-Collins, 1993.

"Catholics of Poland Apologize to Jews." *New York Times*, 28 August 2000, A3.

Chęciński, Michael. *Poland: Communism, Nationalism, Anti-Semitism.* New York: Karz-Cohl Publishing, 1982.

Chrypiński, Vincent C. "Political Change Under Gierek." In *Gierek's Poland*, edited by Adam Bromke and John W. Strong, 36–51. New York: Praeger, 1973.

Cohen, Roger. "The Accommodations of Adam Michnik." *New York Times Magazine*, 7 November 1999, 71–90.

Cviic, Christopher. "The Church." In *Poland: Genesis of a Revolution*, edited by Abraham Brumberg, 92–108. New York: Random House, 1983.

Davies, Norman. *God's Playground: A History of Poland.* Vol. 1. New York: Columbia University Press, 1982.

————. *Heart of Europe: A Short History of Poland.* New York: Oxford University Press, 1986.

de Jonge, Alex. *Stalin, and the Shaping of the Soviet Union.* New York: William Morrow, 1986.

de Weydenthal, Jan B. *The Communists of Poland: An Historical Outline.* Stanford, CA: Hoover Institution Press, 1986.

Dziewanowski, M. K. *The Communist Party of Poland: An Outline of History.* 2nd ed. Cambridge, MA: Harvard University Press, 1976.

—————. *Poland in the Twentieth Century.* New York: Columbia University Press, 1977.

Eckman, Lester Samuel. *Soviet Policy Towards Jews and Israel: 1917–1974.* New York: Shengold, 1974.

Eisler, Jerzy. "March 1968 in Poland." In 1968: *The World Transformed*, edited by Carole Fink, Philipp Gassert, and Detlef Junker, 237–251. Cambridge, UK: Cambridge University Press, 1998.

Ettinger, Shmuel. "Historical and Internal Political Factors in Soviet Anti-Semitism." In *Anti-Semitism in the Soviet Union: Its Roots and Consequences,* edited by Theodore Freedman, 172–178. New York: Anti-Defamation League of B'nai B'rith, 1984.

Friedberg, Maurice. "Antisemitism as a Policy Tool in the Soviet Bloc." In *American Jewish Year Book: 1970,* edited by Morris Fine and Milton Himmelfarb, 123–140. New York: The American Jewish Committee, 1971.

Gilbert, Martin. *The Day The War Ended.* London: HarperCollins, 1995.

Giuliani, Rudolph W. "How Europe Can Stop the Hate." *New York Times,* 18 June 2003, A25.

Golczewski, Frank. "Rural Anti-Semitism in Galicia Before World War I." In *The Jews in Poland*, edited by Chimen Abramsky, Maciej Jachimczyk, and Antony Polonsky, 97–105. Oxford: Basil Blackwell, 1986.

Gomułka, Władysław. "On Zionism." In *Poland Since 1956: Readings and Essays on Polish Government and Politics*, edited by Tadeusz N. Cieplak, 399–401. New York: Twayne, 1972.

Green, Peter S. "Jewish Museum in Poland: More Than a Memorial." *New York Times*, 9 January 2003, A3.

Gross, Jan T. *Neighbors: The Destruction of the Community of Jedwabne, Poland*. Princeton, NJ: Princeton University Press, 2001.

Halecki, Oscar. *A History of Poland*. New York: Dorset, 1992.

Heller, Celia Stopnicka. "'Anti-Zionism' and the Political Struggle within the Elite of Poland." *Journal of Jewish Sociology* 11.2 (December 1969): 133–50.

Henry, Marilyn. "Poland to Expedite Citizenship for 'March' Victims." *Jerusalem Post*, 11 March 1998, 5.

Hoffman, Eva. *Exit Into History: A Journey Through the New Eastern Europe*. New York: Penguin Books, 1993.

Institute of Jewish Affairs. *Anti-Jewish Campaign in Present-Day Poland: Facts, Documents, Press Reports*. 2nd ed. London, 1968.

Johnson, Lonnie R. *Central Europe: Enemies, Neighbors, Friends.* New York: Oxford University Press, 1996.

Karpeles, Gustav. *Jewish Literature and Other Essays.* Freeport, NY: Books for Libraries Press, 1971.

Karpiński, Jakub. *Countdown: The Polish Upheavals of 1956, 1968, 1970, 1976, 1980.* Translated by Olga Amsterdamska and Gene M. Moore. New York: Karz-Cohl, 1982.

Katz, Zev. "After the Six-Day War." In *The Jews in Soviet Russia Since 1917.* 3rd ed., edited by Lionel Kochan, 333–348. New York: Oxford University Press, 1978.

Kaufman, Jonathan. *A Hole in the Heart of the World: The Jewish Experience in Eastern Europe After World War II.* New York: Penguin, 1998.

Kersten, Krystyna. *The Establishment of Communist Rule in Poland, 1943–1948.* Translated by John Micgiel and Michael H. Bernhard. Berkeley, CA: University of California Press, 1991.

Kochan, Lionel. "East European Jewry since 1770." In *The Jewish Enigma,* edited by David Englander, 111–141. New York: Braziller, 1992.

Kołakowski, Leszek. "The Intelligentsia." In *Poland: Genesis of a Revolution,* edited by Abraham Brumberg, 54–67. New York: Random House, 1983.

Korey, William. "The Legal Position of Soviet Jewry: A Historical Enquiry." In *The Jews in Soviet Russia Since 1917*. 3rd ed., edited by Lionel Kochan, 78–105. New York: Oxford University Press, 1978.

Krauthamer, Ky. "Imaginary Jews and Real Anti-Semites: An Interview with Leon Volovici," *Central Europe Review*, 4, no. 5, 15 November 2002, www.ce-review.org/02/5aCER-VoloviciJB.html.

Lendvai, Paul. *Anti-Semitism Without Jews: Communist Eastern Europe*. 1st ed. Garden City, NY: Doubleday, 1971.

Lewis, Bernard. *Semites and Anti-Semites: An Inquiry into Conflict and Prejudice*. New York: Norton, 1986.

Low, Alfred D. *Soviet Jewry and Soviet Policy*. New York: Columbia University Press, 1990.

Mahler, Raphael. *A History of Modern Jewry, 1780–1815*. New York: Schocken, 1971.

Marcus, Jacob R. *The Jew in the Medieval World: A Source Book*, 315–1791. New York: Macmillan, 1938.

Marrus, Michael R. *The Holocaust in History*. Toronto: Lester & Orpen Dennys, 1987.

"Mieczysław Moczar: Polish partisan leader sought supreme power." *The Globe and Mail* (Toronto), 3 November 1986, A16.

Mond, George H. "The Student Rebels in Poland." *East Europe* 18.7 (1969): 2–7.

Myant, Martin. *Poland: A Crisis for Socialism.* London: Lawrence and Wishart, 1982.

"A Nervous New Arrival on the European Union's Block." *The Economist,* 28 August 2003.

Nowak, Jan. "Conflict of Generations in Poland." *East Europe* 17.5 (1968): 13–16.

———. "The Struggle for Party Control in Poland." *East Europe* 17.6 (1968): 2–6.

Parnas, Józef. "Spóźniony List z Wiezienia" ["Belated Letter from Prison"]. *Na Antenie [On the Air]* 10.1 (September 1972): 2.

———. *Sylwetki Moich Nauczycieli [Profiles of My Teachers].* Copenhagen, Denmark: Kronika, 1984.

Pauley, Bruce F. From *Prejudice to Persecution: A History of Austrian Anti-Semitism.* Chapel Hill and London: University of North Carolina Press, 1992.

Pell, Claiborne. "The Pattern of Soviet Anti-Semitism." *East Europe* 20.3 (1971): 18–20.

Podgórecki, Adam. *Polish Society.* Westport, CT: Praeger, 1994.

"Poland and the European Union: Back into the Fold." *The Economist,* 12 June 2003.

Pope John Paul II. *Spiritual Pilgrimage: Texts on Jews and Judaism, 1979–1995.* Edited by Eugene J. Fisher, and Leon Klenicki. New York: Crossroad, 1995.

Prager, Dennis, and Joseph Telushkin. *Why the Jews? The Reason for Antisemitism.* New York: Simon & Schuster, 1983.

Ptakowski, Jerzy. "Behind the Unrest in Poland." *East Europe* 17.4 (1968): 5–11.

———. "Gomułka and His Party." *East Europe* 16.5 (1967): 2–8.

Raina, Peter. *Political Opposition in Poland: 1954–1977.* London: Poets and Painters Press, 1978.

Rapoport, Louis. *Stalin's War Against the Jews: The Doctors' Plot and the Soviet Solution.* New York: Free Press, 1990.

"Rehabilitacja Józefa Parnasa" ["The Rehabilitation of Józef Parnas"]. *Gazeta w Lublinie* 196 /231, Thursday, 7 November 1991, n.pag.

Rosenstein, Neil. *The Unbroken Chain: Biographical Sketches and Genealogy of Illustrious Jewish Families from the 15th–20th Century.* 2 vols. Elizabeth, NJ: Computer Center for Jewish Genealogy, 1990.

Roth, Stephen J. "Anti-Zionism and Anti-Semitism in the USSR." In *Anti-Semitism in the Soviet Union: Its Roots and Consequences,* edited by Theodore Freedman, 160–166. New York: Anti-Defamation League of B'nai B'rith, 1984.

Sachar, Abram Leon. *A History of the Jews.* 5th ed. Rev. New York: Alfred A. Knopf, 1967.

Sachar, Howard M. *The Course of Modern Jewish History.* 3rd ed. Rev. New York: Random House, 1990.

Schapiro, Leonard B. "Antisemitism in the Communist World." *Soviet Jewish Affairs* 9.1 (1979): 42–52.

Schechtman, J. B. "The USSR, Zionism, and Israel." In *The Jews in Soviet Russia Since 1917.* 3rd ed., edited by Lionel Kochan, 106–131. New York: Oxford University Press, 1978.

Sherwin, Byron L. *Sparks Amid The Ashes: The Spiritual Legacy of Polish Jewry,* New York: Oxford University Press, 1997.

Simons, William B., ed. *The Constitutions of the Communist World.* Germantown, MD: Sijthoff & Noordhoff, 1980.

Singer, David, ed. *American Jewish Year Book 1996.* New York: American Jewish Committee, 1997.

Steven, Stewart. *The Poles.* New York: Macmillan, 1982.

"Student Demonstrations in Poland." *East Europe* 17.4 (1968): 2–5.

Sword, Keith. *Deportation and Exile: Poles in the Soviet Union, 1939–48.* London: Macmillan, 1994.

Syrop, Konrad. *Poland in Perspective.* London: Robert Hale, 1982.

Szafar, Tadeusz. "Anti-Semitism: A Trusty Weapon." In *Poland: Genesis of a Revolution,* edited by Abraham Brumberg, 109–122. New York: Random House, 1983.

Szajkowski, Bogdan. *Next to God... Poland: Politics and Religion in Contemporary Poland.* London: Frances Pinter, 1983.

Tagliabue, John. "Chirac to Tackle Anti-Semitism and Muslim Slums of Bitterness." *New York Times*, 18 November 2003, A3.

Taras, Ray. *Poland: Socialist State, Rebellious Nation.* Boulder, CO: Westview Press, 1991.

Tartakower, Arieh. "The Jewish Problem in the Soviet Union." *Jewish Social Studies* 33.4 (October 1971): 285–306.

Terracini, Umberto. "Israel as a factor in Soviet Anti-Semitism." In *Anti-Semitism in the Soviet Union: Its Roots and Consequences*, edited by Theodore Freedman, 167–171. New York: Anti-Defamation League of B'nai B'rith, 1984.

Torańska, Teresa. *"Them": Stalin's Polish Puppets.* Translated by Agnieszka Kolakowska. New York: Harper & Row, 1987.

Tuszyńska, Agata. *Lost Landscapes: In Search of Isaac Bashevis Singer and the Jews of Poland.* Translated by Madeline G. Levine. New York: William Morrow, 1998.

Wasserstein, Bernard. *Vanishing Diaspora: The Jews in Europe Since 1945.* New York: Penguin, 1997.

Weinryb, Bernard D. "Antisemitism in Soviet Russia." In *The Jews in Soviet Russia Since 1917.* 3rd ed., edited by

Lionel Kochan, 300–332. New York: Oxford University Press, 1978.

Weit, Erwin. *Eyewitness: The Autobiography of Gomułka's Interpreter.* Translated by Mary Schofield. London: Andre Deutsch, 1973.

Weizel, Richard. "Donating a Torah to a Warsaw School." *New York Times,* 14 January 2001, 14CN.2.

Wistrich, Robert S. *Antisemitism: The Longest Hatred.* New York: Schocken, 1991.

Index

A

Agnon, Shmuel Yosef, 164
Alexander, King of Poland
(1501–06), 20
Alexander I, Emperor of
Russia (1801–25) and
King of Poland
(1815–25), 63
American Jewish Distribution
Committee, 136
anti-Semitism, 8,
33–34, 71–72, 74
anti-Zionism as, ix–x, 1–5,
36, 58, 135
dangers of, 6–7, 36–37,
39–40, 109–110,
160–161, 164–165
in Communist Poland,
38–42, 48–50, 55,
78–80, 83, 99,
110–116, 123–124,
127–128, 135,
137–139, 147–149,
176n23
in contemporary France,
158–159
in Europe during the late
1960s, 48

in medieval Europe, 15,
70–71, 109
in pre-World War II
Poland, 39, 71–72, 155
in Romania during the
1980s, 48–49, 172n7
in the Soviet Union, 39, 46,
54, 89–90, 92, 97–98,
110, 112–114, 123
Jews as scapegoats, blamed
for society's problems,
68, 82, 93, 96–98,
122–123
Jews' reactions to, 94–95
1967–68 campaign in
Poland, 7–12, 39,
41–42, 47, 70, 73,
80–88, 100–101,
116–117, 127–133
origins of anti-Semitic
beliefs, 37, 70–71, 93,
130
origin of the term, 6
pogroms (attacks on Jews)
in Poland, 31, 38, 96
political and popular sentiments, 36–38; *see also*
pogrom

socialist views of, 35–36,
90–92, 94–95

Zionism as response to,
34–35

anti-Zionist sentiments, *see*
anti-Semitism

Arabs, 5–6, 8, 12, 45–46, 48,
52–54, 69, 85, 129–130

Armia Krajowa, see Home
Army

Auschwitz, Nazi concentration camp, 33, 145, 161

Australia, 116

Austria (Empire), 30, 34, 63,
94–95, 102

B

Baghdad Pact, 52

Bauman, Zygmunt, 69, 116

Belarus, 157

Berman, Jakób, 83, 101

Białystok (Poland), 146, 157

Bierut, Bolesław, 41, 99, 101,
127, 178n22

Birobidzhan, 113–114

Blaszczyk, L.D., 117

Bolesław I, the Brave, King of
Poland (992–1025), 156

Bolesław V, the Chaste, King
of Poland (1243–79), 16

Bolsheviks, 92

Brasch, Rudolph, 67

Brezhnev, Leonid, 51, 133

Brus, Włodzimierz, 98

Buber, Martin, 168n6

Bulgaria, 96

C

Casimir III the Great, King
of Poland (1333–70), 17,
20, 65

Casimir IV, King of Poland
(1446–92), 17, 20

Catherine II the Great,
Empress of Russia
(1762–96), 31

Catholicism, *see* Roman
Catholic Church

Chagall, Marc, 157

Charter of Jewish Liberties
(1264), *see* Kalisz, Statute
of

Chirac, Jacques, 158–159

Chmielnicki, Bogdan, x, 30

Chopin, Fryderyk, 163–164

Cold War, 51

Communism, 35, 61, 65, 95,
100, 103, 110, 112, 130,
133, 136–137, 141, 143,
145, 164

Conrad, Joseph, 163

Constitution of 3 May 1791,
152

Coordinating Committee of
Jewish Organizations,
146

Copenhagen (Denmark), xiii,
123–124

Copernicus, Nicolas, 27, 163

Cosmopolitans (Communist
euphemism for Jews), 80,
85–86, 89, 92, 96, 110

Cossacks, x, 30

Council of Four Lands, 24, 26

Cracow (Poland), 15, 17–20, 24, 26–27, 31, 38, 43, 62–66, 105, 106, 117, 141–143, 146–147, 157, 163

The Crusades, 15–16

Cuba, 48

Curie-Skłodowska, Marie, 163

Cyrankiewicz, Józef, 106

Czechoslovakia, 1–2, 59, 96, 118, 128, 132–133

Częstochowa (Poland), 105, 149

D

Dajczgewand, Józef, 81–82

Denmark, xiii, 123–124, 180n27

Dmowski, Roman, 156

Doctors' Plot, 92–93, 135

Dubček, Alexander, 1, 133

Dziady (Forefathers' Eve), 41, 61–63, 73, 84, 131

E

Edels, Rabbi Samuel Eliezer, 26

Egypt, 45–46, 52

Endecja (pre-WWII National Democratic Party), 39, 156

England, 109, 163

The Enlightenment, 31

European Union, xii, 143–144, 152–154, 156, 158–160, 163

F

Ferband, see Jewish Socio-Cultural Society (*Towarzystwo Społeczno-Kulturalne Żydów*)

Fifth Column, 47, 70, 84, 93, 130–131
    origin of term, 91

First World War, xi, 34–35, 95

Folk anti-Semitism, *see* Anti-Semitism

Folksshtimme, 81

France, 95, 109, 158–159

Franco, Francisco, 91

Franz Joseph I, Emperor of Austria (1848–1916), 30

Frederick II, Holy Roman Emperor (1220–50), 16

G

Galicia, 24, 30, 157, 164

Gazeta Wyborcza, 136

Gdańsk (Poland), 134, 146

Gdynia (Poland), 134

Gehry, Frank, 151

Geremek, Bronisław, 138

Germany, 15, 37–38, 47, 72, 94–96, 99, 102–103, 105, 109, 156–157, 176n23

Gierek, Edward, 68, 123, 132, 134–136, 179n22

Giuliani, Rudolph, 158

Golan Heights, 45

Gomułka, Władysław, 4, 9, 11–12, 40–42, 44, 47, 57–61, 63, 65–66, 68, 70,

72–73, 75–77, 79–80,
83–88, 91, 98–102,
104–107, 112, 123, 127,
129, 131–136, 179n22
Gomułka, Zofia (wife), 83
Górecki, Henryk, 164
Górecki, Jan, 81
Górecki, Wiktor (son of Jan),
81
Gottwald, Klement, 97
Great Britain, 45, 51–52
Gromyko, Andrei, 51
Grunwald Patriotic Union,
127, 137–138

H

Halbersztadt, Jerzy, 151
Hasidism, 142, 157
Herzl, Theodore, 35
HIAS (Hebrew Sheltering
and Immigrant Aid Soci-
ety), 116
Hitler, Adolf, 37–38, 95, 125
Holocaust, 1–3, 33, 35, 38,
40, 94, 96, 110, 125,
145–149, 176n23
Home Army, *Armia Krajowa*
(AK) (Poland's wartime
military forces), 118
Hungarian Revolution (1956),
41, 59
Hungary, 48, 96

I

India, 117
Industrial Revolution, 31
Inquisition, 16

Intelligentsia, xi, 42, 60, 98,
106, 156
Iran, 52
Iraq, 52
Ireland, 102
Israel, 1, 5–6, 8, 12, 23, 35,
40, 45–55, 69–70, 73, 85,
92, 102, 106, 114–116,
120, 129–130, 145, 164,
178n15, *see also* Zionism
Isserles, Rabbi Moses, 26
Izvestia, 93

J

Jabotinsky, Ze'ev (Vladimir),
178n15
Jadwiga, Polish monarch
(1383–99), 18
Jagiellonian Dynasty
(1386–1572), 17, 22,
27–28, 64–65, 145, 152,
156–157, 160
Jagiellonian University, 17,
27, 62, 64–66, 147
Jarosław (Poland), 24
Jaruzelski, Wojciech, 179n22
Jasna Góra (Catholic shrine
in Częstochowa), 105,
149
Jedwabne Pogrom, 38, 149,
151, 170n9
Jewish Historical Institute
(Warsaw), 147
Jewish Socio-Cultural Society
(*Towarzystwo Społeczno-
Kulturalne Żydów*), 146
Jews, 1–2, 6, 15–17, 20,
33–34, 145–151

achievements in Poland,
19, 21–26, 28–29, 156,
165
attraction to socialist
movements, 94–95
Catholic Church's response
to the oppression of
the Jews in Poland,
106–107, 137, 148, 161
decline in status, 26,
29–30, 32, 47, 49,
67–69, 79, 84–88, 99,
109–110, 114, 128, 130
forced emigration from
Poland after March
1968, 114–116
in the Austrian Empire, 30
in France, 157–159
in Poland, xii–xiii, 2–4,
8–11, 15–32, 33–40,
49–50, 55, 68–69,
79–80, 84–88, 98,
100–101, 114–125,
127–128, 135–137,
145–151, 156, 165
in pre-revolutionary Russia
and Soviet Union,
30–31, 34, 39–40, 46,
50–51, 53–55, 80, 89,
91–93, 97–98, 113–114
in Romania, 48–49, 172n7
migration to Poland,
15–16, 18, 20
persecution of, 2, 5, 7–9,
15, 20, 29–31, 33–36,
38–40, 46–47, 54–55,
57–58, 67–68, 72–73,
79–82, 90–93, 96–98,
100–101, 112,
114–117, 128,
140–141, 149, *see also*
anti-Semitism; Holo-
caust
population figures, 20, 34,
40, 49, 69, 103, 112,
114, 137–138, 146
religious and cultural identity, 17, 20–21, 29,
70–71, 109, 176n23
John I Albert, King of Poland
(1492–1501), 20
John Paul II, Pope, 33, 106,
161
Jordan, 45
Joskowicz, Rabbi Pinchas
Menachem, 145

K

Kahal (assembly of elders),
23–24
Kalisz, Statute of, 16–17
Kaminska, Ida, 116
Kania, Stanisław, 179n22
Katowice (Poland), 146
Katzenellenbogen, Rabbi
Samuel Judah, 21, 155
Katzenellenbogen, Rabbi Saul
Wahl, 21–22, 168n6
Katz-Suchy, Julius, 117
Kehillah, 23, 146
Khrushchev, Nikita, 51–52,
59, 67, 90, 97–99
Kielce Pogrom, 38, 96
Kieślowski, Krzysztof, 164
Koch, Erich, 125
Kołakowski, Leszek, 61, 116

Kraków, see Cracow (Poland)
Kremlin, xi, 51, 57, 59, 75,
    107, 133
Kurier Polski, 81
Kuroń, Jacek, 62, 64,
    121–122, 136–137
Kwaśniewski, Aleksander,
    137, 149, 171n9

L

Lasota, Irena, 81
Lauder-Morasha School
    (Warsaw), 147
Lemberg (Galicia), *see* Lwów
    (Poland)
Lenin, Vladimir, 51, 91–93
Lithuania, 17–18, 20, 24,
    26–28, 157, 168n4
Łódź (Poland), 117, 146
Lublin (Poland), 24, 62,
    118–119, 146, 157
Luporini, Cesare, 73
Łutosławski, Witold, 164
Lviv (Ukraine), *see* Lwów
    (Poland)
Lvov, *see* Lwów (Poland)
Lwów (Poland), 24, 157,
    176n23

M

Maastricht Treaty, 153
Maharsha, see Edels, Rabbi
    Samuel Eliezer
Marr, Wilhelm, 6
Malenkov, Georgy, 52
Małopolska, see Galicia

Mapai (Israel Workers'
    Party), 52
March 1968, 5, 41, 61–67, 80,
    84–88, 106, 114,
    116–117, 120–121, 125,
    128, 131–133, 137
Marie Curie-Skłodowska
    University, 118–119
Marx, Karl, 168n6
Marxism, 36, 66, 95, 127, 133
Meir, Golda, 45, 54
Mendelssohn, Rabbi Moses,
    168n6
Mendelssohn-Bartholdy,
    Felix, 168n6
Mensheviks, 92
Michnik, Adam, 62, 64,
    81–82, 107, 121, 136,
    138, 176n23
Mickiewicz, Adam, 41, 43, 61,
    73, 131
Mieszko I, Prince (c.960–92),
    102, 156
Miłosz, Czesław, 164
Minc, Hilary, 83, 101
Minsk (Belarus), 157
Moczar, Mieczysław, 9, 12,
    42, 44, 57–58, 68–70,
    72–81, 83, 86–88, 93,
    98–102, 106–107, 112,
    120, 123, 125, 127,
    129–135, 138
Modzelewski, Karol, 62, 121
Mola, Emilio, 91
Morawski, Stefan, 116–117
Moscow (Russia), 52, 54, 59,
    88, 110, 118
Muscovites, 90, 99–101, 130

N

Naples, 109
Nasser, Gamal Abdel, 45, 47,
  52
nationalism, 32–34, 48–50,
  77–78, 80, 87, 89, 94–95,
  132, 161
NATO, xi, 52, 143, 153
Nazarewicz, Col. (Polish military prosecutor), 121
Nazism, 2–3, 33–34, 38, 40,
  42, 64, 72, 76, 79, 90, 99,
  103, 110, 112, 118, 125,
  145–146, 151, 176n23
Nazi-Soviet Pact (1939), 38
Nowe Drogi, 82

O

Ochab, Edward, 101, 135,
  178n22

P

Paderewski, Ignacy, 164
Padua (Italy), 21
Pakistan, 52
Pale of Settlement, 30, 95
Pankrac prison (Prague), 97
Parnas, Józef, xiii, 9,
  117–125, 137, 180n27
Partisan faction of General
  Moczar, 42, 57–58, 68,
  73, 76–79, 84, 87–89, 99,
  101, 106, 117, 120, 127,
  129, 131–132, 134; *see
  also ZBoWiD*; Moczar,
  Mieczysław

wartime partisan fighters,
  90, 99–100, 118
Paul VI, Pope, 105
PAX Organization, 77, 81,
  104
Pell, Claiborne (U.S. Senator),
  114
Penderecki, Krzysztof, 164
Peter I, the Great, Emperor
  of Russia (1682–1725),
  112
The Pianist (motion picture),
  3, 151, 167n2; *see also*
  Szpilman, Władysław
Piasecki, Bolesław, 77, 104
Piast Dynasty (966–1138,
  1305–1370), 17, 156, 159
Piłsudski, Józef, 156
Podolia, 24
pogrom, 31, 96, 128, 142,
  171n9; *see also* Jedwabne;
  Kielce
Polański, Roman, 3, 151,
  164–165, 167n2
Polin, 18, 23
Polish-Lithuanian Republic
  (1569–1795), x, 27–28,
  152, 155
Polish October (1956), 41, 66,
  100, 127
Polish United Workers' Party
  (PUWP), 5, 8–9, 40, 42,
  44, 57, 68, 70, 87, 99,
  106, 120, 133–135,
  178n22
Polish Workers' Party, 75
political Zionism, *see* Zionism
Polityka, 80

Portugal, 109
Posen, *see* Poznań (Poland)
Poznań (Poland), 24, 62, 157
Prague (Czechoslovakia), 65,
 97
Prague Spring (1968), 1, 66,
 133
Pravda, 80, 93
Protestantism, 27–28, 155
Prussia, x, 30–31, 34, 63
Przemyśl (Poland), 146
PUWP, *see* Polish United
 Workers' Party

R

Radziwill, Prince Nicholas,
 21–22, 155
Rakowski, Mieczysław, 80
Red Army, 38, 59, 112, 128
The Reformation, 27
Rema, see Isserles, Rabbi
 Moses
The Renaissance, 27, 31
Revisionist Zionism, *see* Zion-
 ism
Roman Catholic Church,
 27–30, 61, 77, 90,
 102–107, 132, 138,
 148–149
Romania, 48–49, 59, 96,
 172n7
Ronald S. Lauder Foundation,
 147
Rovno Brigade (unit of
 Poland's Home Army
 [AK]), 118, 125
Rovno (Ukraine), 125
Rubenstein, Helena, 168n6

Rubinstein, Artur, 164–165
Russell, Bertrand, 73
Russia, x, 2, 24, 30, 34, 39,
 45, 48, 50–51, 63, 69, 77,
 89, 91–92, 95, 97,
 100–102, 112, 118, 123,
 128, 131; *see also* Soviet
 Union
Russian Revolution, 91

S

scapegoat (Jews as), 32, 36,
 42, 55, 67–70, 82–83, 89,
 92–94, 97, 122, 128, 130,
 134, 161, 165
 attributes for role of, 69
 origin of term, 67–68
Schaff, Adam, 117
Schudrich, Rabbi Michael,
 146–147
Second World War, x–xi,
 2–4, 14, 33, 35–36,
 38–40, 50, 64, 80, 89, 92,
 94–95, 103, 110, 113,
 118, 123, 128, 130, 137,
 147, 149, 151, 154, 156,
 176n23
sejm (Polish parliament), 26,
 28
Siberia, 39, 113
Sigismund I the Elder, King
 of Poland (1506–48), 17,
 20
Sigismund II Augustus, King
 of Poland (1548–72),
 22–23, 28, 152
Sigismund III, King of
 Poland (1587–1632), 22

Singer, Isaac Bashevis, 164–165
Six-Day War (1967), 5, 8–10, 12, 36, 45–48, 50, 55, 89, 106, 120, 128–129
Slansky, Rudolf, 96–97
Słowo Powszechne, 81
Smolar, Aleksander (son of Gregorz), 81
Smolar, Grzegorz Hersch, 81, 116
Socialism, 41, 53, 67, 77, 86, 91, 94, 104, 127–128, 156
Solidarity (Polish trade union and political party), 125, 133, 136–138
Soviet Union, ix, 1, 8–9, 11–12, 36, 40–41, 45–46, 48, 50–55, 57–59, 65–67, 74, 77, 80, 83, 88–93, 97–99, 110–114, 118, 124, 129–130, 132–134; *see also* Russia
Spain, 109, 153
Stalin, Joseph, 9, 39, 50–51, 54, 69, 89–94, 96–99, 102, 110–114, 118, 123, 135
Stalinism, 93, 96–97, 100–101, 127, 132, 176
Statute of General Toleration (1573), 28
Statute of Kalisz (1264), *see* Kalisz, Statute of
Statute of Wiślica (1346), *see* Wiślica, Statute of
Stefan Batory, King of Poland (1575–1586), 21

Sweden, x
Syria, 45–46, 52
Szczecin (Poland), 134, 146
szlachta (Polish nobility), 28, 163, 169n13
Szlajfer, Henryk, 62, 64, 81
Szpilman, Władysław, 3–4, 164–165
Szymborska, Wisława, 164

T

Technocrats, 68, 134
Terracini, Umberto, 53
Tito, Marshal (Josip Broz), 47
totalitarianism, xii–xiii, 1, 4, 6–7, 54, 59, 72, 117, 133, 145
Treaty of Versailles, 34
Trybuna Ludu, 81–82, 116
Turkey, x, 52
Tuwim, Julian, 138
Tygodnik Powszechny, 106

U

Ukraine, x, 125, 157, 176
Union of Jewish Religious Communities (*Związek Kongregacji Wyznania Mojzeszowego*), 146
Union of Lublin (1569), 28
Union of Mielnik (1501), 20
United States of America, 45, 51, 66, 92
University of Cracow, *see* Jagiellonian University
University of Łódź, 117

University of Padua, 21
USSR, *see* Soviet Union

V

Vaad Arba Aratzot, see Council
of Four Lands
Vilna, *see* Wilno (Poland)
Vilnius (Lithuania), *see* Wilno
(Poland)
Vitebsk (Belarus), 157
Volhynia, 24, 125
Vyshinsky, Andrei, 123

W

Wahl, Saul, *see* Katzenellen-
bogen, Rabbi Saul Wahl
Wajda, Andrzej, 164
Wałęsa, Lech, 133
Walichnowski, Tadeusz, 79
Warsaw (Poland), 3, 15, 41,
61–64, 81–82, 84, 99,
111, 114, 116–117, 121,
125, 133, 136–137, 141,
144–148, 151, 157, 164
Warsaw Ghetto, 147, 150
Warsaw Pact, 133
Warsaw University, 61–63,
66, 69, 81, 116–117, 147
Warszawa, see Warsaw
(Poland)
Werfel, Katarzyna (daughter
of Roman), 82
Werfel, Roman, 82, 101
Wieniawski, Henryk,
164–165
Więź, 106
Wilno (Poland), 24, 157

Wiślica, Statute of, 17
Władysław II Jagiełło, Grand
Duke of Lithuania
(1386–1434), 18
Wojtyła, Cardinal Archbishop
Karol, *see* John Paul II,
Pope
Wolak, Edward, xiii, 180n27
Wrocław (Poland), 49, 114,
117, 146
Wysłouch, Bolesław, 156
Wyszyński, Cardinal Stefan,
Primate of Poland,
104–106, 138

Y

Yugoslavia, 47–48, 59

Z

Zambrowski, Roman,
100–101
Zarzycka, Ewa, 82
Zawadzki, Aleksander, 101
ZBoWiD (Union of Fighters
for Freedom and Democ-
racy), 42, 77–78, 135
Zionism, 8, 35, 45–48, 51, 54,
80, 84, 87, 91; *see also*
Israel
anti-Zionist sentiments, *see*
anti-Semitism
political Zionism, 35
Revisionist Zionism,
178n15

About the Author

Arthur J. Wolak has traveled extensively in Poland and other European countries for personal interest and research. The son of Holocaust survivors, Arthur was raised in Vancouver, Canada, where he earned his bachelor of arts degree with first class honors from the University of British Columbia. He holds a master of arts from California State University, an MBA from the University of Colorado, and a certificate in social change in post-Communist Poland from Warsaw University. He is currently working on his doctorate.